LEADERSHIP

PROMISES FOR YOUR WORK WEEK

JOHN C.
MAXWELL

COUNTRYMAN®

Nashville, Tennessee

TABLE OF CONTENTS

INTRODUCTION

L eadership is essential to accomplishing every goal in life, and as a leader, you must grow in order to succeed. Think you're not a leader? Think again. First and foremost, you lead yourself. Then, through your influence—official or unofficial, personal or professional—you lead others. You even show leadership through the attitude and ethics with which you follow those with authority over you.

You are a leader, and this book is for you. It's a collection of fifty–two devotionals following a new theme every week. Each chapter includes a promise that God has made to leaders, a promise good leaders make to their teams, a quick lesson, and a thought or activity to help carry you through the week.

Leadership Promises for Your Work Week provides biblical principles to help you develop as a leader, build stronger team players, and develop successful teams. Don't start your week without it!

GOD'S PROMISE
TO LEADERS

The LORD shows mercy and is kind.
He does not become angry quickly, and he has great love.
He will not always accuse us,
and he will not be angry forever.
He has not punished us as our sins should be punished;
he has not repaid us for the evil we have done.
The LORD has mercy on those who respect him,
as a father has mercy on his children.

PSALM 103:8–9, 13 (NCV)

A LEADER'S PROMISE
TO THE TEAM

I AM HUMBLY AWARE OF HOW
MUCH I'VE ALREADY BEEN FORGIVEN,
AND I WILL CONTINUE OWNING UP
TO MY MISTAKES.

WEEK 1

ACCEPT RESPONSIBILITY

And David said to God, "Was it not I who commanded the people to be numbered? I am the one who has sinned and done evil indeed; but these sheep, what have they done? Let Your hand, I pray, O LORD my God, be against me and my father's house, but not against Your people that they should be plagued."

1 CHRONICLES 21:17

Times of failure not only reveal a leader's true character, but also present opportunities for significant leadership lessons.

After a major victory over the Philistines, King David made a major mistake. The king stopped trusting God for the defense of his nation and undertook a census to measure his military power. David's willingness to take responsibility for his foolish action demonstrated his depth of character. He repented and accepted punishment from the hand of God, trusting in the grace of God. Even so, David's error snuffed out the lives of seventy thousand Israelites. When leaders mess up, many people suffer.

Many leaders attempt to hide failures, blame others, or run from God. But David admitted his failure and repented. Although he faced many difficulties, David worked to restore his relationship with God and did whatever he could to minimize the consequences of his failure in the lives of others.

The Maxwell Leadership Bible

LIFTING THE LID

"Also, in time past, when Saul was king over us,
you were the one who led Israel out and brought them in;
and the LORD said to you, 'You shall shepherd My people Israel,
and be ruler over Israel'."

2 SAMUEL 5:2

Why did Saul fail as Israel's king, while David succeeded? The answer can be found in the Law of the Lid. Leadership ability is the lid that determines a person's level of effectiveness. And to reach the highest level of effectiveness, you have to raise the lid on your leadership ability. David had many lids on his life, but they did not stop him:

1. His family
2. His leader
3. His background
4. His youthfulness and inexperience

Ultimately, David became a great leader—yet not because he lacked limitations in life. He achieved much because he became a lid lifter.

Every leader has lids on his life; nobody is born without them. And they don't disappear when a person receives a title, achieves a position, or gets invested with power. The issue is not whether you have lids, but what you are going to do about them.

The Maxwell Leadership Bible

Following in Your Footsteps

*So Aaron and his sons did all the things that
the LORD had commanded by the hand of Moses.*

LEVITICUS 8:36

Aaron, like many leaders through history, received a divine calling. God chose Aaron and his sons to serve as Israel's priests and charged them with carrying out rituals and sacrifices on behalf of all Israelites. Scripture gives meticulous detail to their ordination and calling. Their conduct was to be beyond reproach—God made it crystal clear that failure to uphold His established guidelines would result in death.

Despite his high calling, Aaron at times struggled with his authority. He once caved in to the depraved wishes of the people and led Israel in a pagan worship service, an abomination that led to the deaths of many Israelites. Aaron had been set apart for God's service, but on that occasion, he chose to live and lead otherwise.

The failure of a leader usually results in consequences far more grave that the fall of a nonleader; on the day Aaron failed, "about three thousand men of the people [died]" (Exodus 32:28). When leaders fall, followers also pay the price.

The Maxwell Leadership Bible

THIS WEEK: Are you letting any of the lids on your life hold you down? Who has suffered because of your failures? Ask key people for forgiveness, and see if there's any way to repair the damage.

GOD'S PROMISE
TO LEADERS

The mouth of the righteous speaks wisdom,
And his tongue talks of justice.
The law of his God is in his heart;
None of his steps shall slide.

PSALM 37:30–31

A LEADER'S PROMISE
TO THE TEAM

I KNOW HOW MUCH I NEED GOD'S HELP,
AND I TURN TO HIM DAILY
FOR COUNSEL AND ENCOURAGEMENT.

ACKNOWLEDGE GOD'S ROLE

*When I consider Your heavens, the work of Your fingers,
the moon and the stars, which You have ordained, what is man
that You are mindful of him, and the son of man that You
visit him? For You have made him a little lower than the angels,
and You have crowned him with glory and honor. You have
made him to have dominion over the works of Your hands;
You have put all things under his feet . . . O LORD, our Lord,
how excellent is Your name in all the earth!*

PSALM 8:3–6, 9

Have you ever asked, "When does a leader's confidence become arrogance? What does humility look like in a leader's life?" Psalm 8 shows leaders how to balance their identity with their self–esteem. Consider how David maintains both confidence and humility.

1. David sees his own weakness and humanity. David realizes that in the sweep of the galaxy, man accounts for only a very small part.

2. David sees his God–given position and privileges. David knows that God has made humankind a little lower than Himself.

3. David sees a balance by giving all the glory to God. David closes the psalm the way he began. He magnifies the Lord and gives Him the credit for the good that has come from his life and leadership.

The Maxwell Leadership Bible

SECURITY IS FOUND IN GOD, NOT IN FOLLOWERS

Unless the LORD builds the house, they labor in vain who build it; unless the LORD guards the city, the watchman stays awake in vain.

PSALM 127:1

Unless God remains at the center of your efforts, you labor in vain. Whether we lead in the military, in construction, or sit behind a desk, we cannot fight, build, or plan well enough to gain anything permanent. Smart leaders not only include God in their strategy, they place Him at its center. Consider the following list of rules regarding security and people.

1. People cannot provide permanent security for a leader.

2. Leaders should never put their emotional health in the hands of someone else.

3. Spiritual and emotional health requires the truth.

4. Leaders must remember that hurting people naturally hurt people.

5. Trouble arises when leaders depend on people to do what only God can do.

In trouble? Turn to God. "I waited patiently for the LORD; and He inclined to me, and heard my cry. He also brought me up out of a horrible pit, out of the miry clay, and set my feet upon a rock, and established my steps" (Psalm 40:1–2). God is rich in grace and mercy. He not only forgives, but restores and redeems. When times of trouble arrive—even trouble we bring on ourselves—we must turn to God and wait patiently for His help. He'll never fail us.

The Maxwell Leadership Bible

GUIDE THE WAY

I will instruct you and teach you in the way you should go;
I will guide you with My eye.

PSALM 32:8

Leaders must closely observe the flock for its needs and problems. God expects spiritual leaders to serve as guides. A guide takes a person or group safely to a planned destination. The Hebrew word for "guide" gives us several clues as to what God expects from those He uses as leaders. A guide . . .

is a spiritual head who unites and directs people in their walk with God.

takes people on the straight path that leads to fellowship with God.

gives accurate and godly counsel to those who need it.

leads with gentleness and trustworthiness, making others feel safe.

bases his or her direction on the Spirit and the Word of God.

The Maxwell Leadership Bible

THIS WEEK: Meditate daily on Psalm 23. Then notice what happens to your stress level. Psalm 23 reminds us of what God alone can control and what we can control. It distinguishes between problems (things we can change) and facts (things we cannot change). It defines God as our . . .

possession	provision	peace
pardon	partner	preparation
praise	paradise	

The Maxwell Leadership Bible

GOD'S PROMISE
TO LEADERS

If my people who are called by my name
will humble themselves and pray and seek my face
and turn from their wicked ways,
I will hear from heaven and will forgive their
sins and heal their land. I will listen to
every prayer made in this place.

2 CHRONICLES 7:14–15 (NLT)

A LEADER'S PROMISE
TO THE TEAM

I UNDERSTAND THAT THE QUALITY
OF MY LEADERSHIP SPRINGS FROM THE
QUALITY OF MY HEART. I WILL GUARD MY HEART.

═══ WEEK 3 ═══

ACHIEVE VICTORY OVER SELF

Surely the princes of Zoan are fools; Pharaoh's wise counselors give foolish counsel . . . Let them know what the LORD of hosts has purposed against Egypt. The princes of Zoan have become fools; the princes of Noph are deceived; they have also deluded Egypt, those who are the mainstay of its tribes.

ISAIAH 19:11–13

M ost natural leaders don't aspire to be great leaders; they aspire to be great persons. Personal qualifications lead to leadership qualifications. When leaders lead their own lives well, others naturally want to follow.

Consider Mother Teresa of Calcutta, India. It's doubtful she ever said, "I am going to set out to be a great leader!" Yet that is what she became by determining to be the person God created her to be.

If we want our leadership to last, we must pay attention to four crucial elements:

Character enables us to do what is right even when it seems difficult.

Perspective enables us to understand what must happen to reach a goal.

Courage enables us to initiate and take risks to step out toward a worthy goal.

Favor enables us to attract and empower others to join us in the cause.

The Maxwell Leadership Bible

WIN WITHIN

How does a leader seek victory over self? Consider how King Josiah conquered himself (2 Chronicles 34:31).

1. *He remained open and teachable.* Josiah humbled himself. He departed from the ways of his arrogant father and sought God.

2. *He removed obstacles carried forward from the past.* Josiah swept the country clean of idols.

3. *He realized what he needed to give and gave it.* Victory always carries a personal cost. For Josiah, that meant repairing the temple and reinstating the Passover.

4. *He recognized the key to victory.* For Josiah, the key to victory was repentance.

5. *He retained a personal commitment to succeed.* People never become more committed than their leader. Josiah's personal commitment inspired the people to be faithful despite their evil desires and history.

What qualities should every leader possess? Psalm 15 lists many of the necessary traits. David pictures a godly leader as one who . . .

possesses integrity.

does not participate in gossip.

does not harm others.

speaks out against wrong.

honors others who walk in truth.

keeps their word even at personal cost.

isn't greedy to gain at the expense of others.

is strong and stable.

The Maxwell Leadership Bible

ALARM BELLS FOR LEADERS

Do not be deceived, God is not mocked; for whatever a man sows, that he will also reap. For he who sows to his flesh will of the flesh reap corruption, but he who sows to the Spirit will of the Spirit reap everlasting life. And let us not grow weary while doing good, for in due season we shall reap if we do not lose heart. Therefore, as we have opportunity, let us do good to all, especially to those who are of the household of faith.

GALATIANS 6:7–10

We can't pull a fast one on God. He sees all and cannot be deceived. To ensure that we live by this truth, seek others to act as your "alarm bells" and ask you tough questions, such as the following:

Is your personal walk with God up–to–date?

Are you keeping your priorities straight?

Are you asking yourself the hard questions?

Are you accountable to someone in authority?

Are you sensitive to what God is saying to the whole body of Christ?

Are you over–concerned with building your image?

Do you put more stock in "events" rather than "process"?

Are you a loner in your leadership and personal life?

Are you aware and honest about your weaknesses?

Is your calling constantly before you?

The Maxwell Leadership Bible

THIS WEEK: Consider what victories over yourself you still need to achieve, What's your battle plan? What victories are already accomplished or well in hand?

GOD'S PROMISE
TO LEADERS

If we say we have no sin, we are fooling ourselves,
and the truth is not in us. But if we confess
our sins, he will forgive our sins, because we can
trust God to do what is right. He will
cleanse us from all the wrongs we have done.

1 JOHN 1:8–9 (NCV)

A LEADER'S PROMISE
TO THE TEAM

I TAKE MY CHARACTER SERIOUSLY.
MY MORAL COMPASS IS SET. SOMETIMES I
DO FALL, HOWEVER, AND WHEN THAT HAPPENS,
I'LL APOLOGIZE AND WORK QUICKLY
TO REPAIR THE DAMAGE DONE BY MY MISTAKES.

BALANCE YOUR GIFTS WITH CHARACTER

For people who hate discipline and only get more stubborn,
there'll come a day when life tumbles in and they break,
but by then it'll be too late to help them.

PROVERBS 29:1 (MSG)

How many leaders have ruined their lives and damaged the lives of others through immorality? Character has become a crucial issue today precisely because of the myriad leaders in the political, business, and religious worlds who have fallen morally. Leaders need to remember that they influence many others beyond themselves; they never fall in a vacuum. They also need to realize that replacing fallen leaders is a slow and difficult process.

So how can we guard against falling? First, we must take care not to emphasize the gifts of a leader over his or her character. We have an unhealthy tendency to see and reward the gift more than the character; but both are to be developed. We must strike the following balance if we are to finish well:

What I Am—Humble, Convicted, Visionary

What I Do—Rely on God, Do the Right Thing, Set Goals

What I Gain—Power from God, High Morale, Credibility

The Maxwell Leadership Bible

Even leaders gifted with tremendous natural leadership can have a very difficult time, especially with issues of character. That was true for Jacob. From the very beginning he wielded great influence. Wealthy, strong, and blessed with a large family, Jacob seemed to have everything. But a leader who goes his own way cannot be an effective instrument in God's hands. God had to break Jacob to make him useful (Genesis 32:24–25). In the breaking process, Jacob—the deceiving "heel–catcher"—became Israel, a "prince of God" who purposed to serve God rather than himself.

Natural leaders often need to be broken. Consider your natural ability to lead a gift from God, but your character a gift to present back to God. Every time you stand up under the weight of adversity, you are being prepared, as Jacob was, to better serve God and lead people.

Warning signs. Throughout the book of Esther, Haman gives us a clear picture of a leader out of control.
1. He lost joy over little problems.
2. He needed friends to build his self–image.
3. His greed made him unhappy.
4. He listened to the wrong people.
5. He thought too highly of himself.
6. He set himself up for a fall.
7. He reaped what he sowed.

The Maxwell Leadership Bible

REPAIR CHARACTER FAULTS

Now about that time Herod the king stretched out
his hand to harass some from the church. Then he killed James
the brother of John with the sword. And because he saw
that it pleased the Jews, he proceeded further to seize Peter also.

ACTS 12:1–3

Ego drove King Herod of Paul's day, just as it had driven his father and grandfather. They all desperately lacked character. Herod's lack of character provides many examples of what not to do as a leader:

1. He mistreated his own citizens.
2. He made decisions based on popularity.
3. He acted irrationally in difficult times.
4. He harbored anger toward others.
5. He sought power out of insecurity.
6. He projected an infallible image.
7. He was blinded by his ego.

To improve your character and build a solid foundation of your own leadership, you must:

Identify where you're weak or have taken shortcuts.

Look for patterns.

Apologize to those you've wronged.

Stay teachable and rebuild.

The Maxwell Leadership Bible

THIS WEEK: Pay particular attention to your character. In what ways are you living up to the standards to which you aspire? How are you falling short? How can you improve? What character victories have you had recently?

GOD'S PROMISE
TO LEADERS

Who are those who fear the LORD?
He will show them the path they should choose.
They will live in prosperity,
and their children will inherit the Promised Land.
Friendship with the LORD is reserved
for those who fear him.
With them he shares the secrets of his covenant.

PSALM 25:12–14 (NLT)

A LEADER'S PROMISE
TO THE TEAM

I RESPECT GOD. I SEEK TO BE HIS FRIEND
AND LIVE IN HIS WISDOM. THIS EMPHASIS WILL
MAKE ME A BETTER LEADER FOR OUR TEAM.

BE A MENTOR

So it was, whenever Moses went out to the tabernacle,
that all the people rose, and each man stood at his tent door
and watched Moses until he had gone into the tabernacle.

EXODUS 33:8

M odeling provides the basis of all true leadership. Leaders must set the example for their followers. The number one management principle in the world is this: People do what people see.

Moses demonstrated this truth. The people watched him as he spent time with God, interceding for them in intimate, personal communion—and it changed them more than any sermon could have. If you want to enjoy an intimate relationship with God, as Moses did, you must practice what he did:

1. Separate yourself regularly.
2. Seek God with all your heart.
3. Risk being watched and scrutinized.
4. Learn to listen and obey God's voice.
5. Enter covenant partnership with God.

Remember, the number one management principle in the world is, "People do what people see." If they want to succeed, leaders must incarnate the life they desire in their followers.

The Maxwell Leadership Bible

PLAY FAVORITES

One of the biggest mistakes a coach can make is to believe that he must treat all of his players the same. Coaches are hired to win—not to make everyone happy or give everyone equal time, money, or resources. Every player must be given support and encouragement, but poor or mediocre performance should not be rewarded the same as the outstanding contributions.

Great coaches give opportunities, resources, and playing time according to players' performance records. The greater the performer, the greater the opportunities. When you have a player like Michael Jordan, you want to put the ball in his hands as often as possible.

When you aren't sure about a player's performance level, especially with a "rookie," give that player frequent but small opportunities to determine his or her caliber of play, and that will show you how to respond.

Developing the Leaders Around You

See the heart and the potential. Every person carries the seed of success. To find it, you have to look at their gifts, temperament, passions, successes, joys, and opportunities. And once you find that seed, you need to fertilize it with encouragement and water it with opportunity. Remember . . .

Everyone wants to feel worthwhile.

Everyone needs and responds to encouragement.

People are naturally motivated.

People buy into the person before buying into their leadership.

The more you understand people, the greater your chance of success in mentoring.

Your Road Map for Success

SHARE THE GAME PLAN

*And He said to them, "Go into all the world
and preach the gospel to every creature."*

MARK 16:15

Every good coach I've watched has worked from a game plan. He's got one not only for each individual game, but a plan for the development of the whole team over the course of the current and upcoming seasons. Once the game plan has been drawn up, he then communicates it to his team on an almost continual basis. Paul "Bear" Bryant, the legendary Alabama football coach, had five points that explained what he believed a coach should do.

1. Tell players what you expect of them.
2. Give players an opportunity to perform.
3. Let players know how they're getting along.
4. Instruct and empower players when they need it.
5. Reward players according to their contribution.

The process must begin with communicating the game plan. That is the key to productivity. But it must continue with the exchange of information. As Sydney J. Harris said, information is "giving out" while communication is "getting through." When there is interactive communication between the team leader and his people, it empowers them to succeed.

Developing the Leaders Around You

THIS WEEK: Psalm 119 is the longest chapter in the Bible, and a main theme is the writer's passion for God's mentoring. Read Psalm 119, and consider how your passion for God's mentoring compares to the writer's.

GOD'S PROMISE
TO LEADERS

*And Christ gave gifts to people—he made some
to be apostles, some to be prophets, some to go and
tell the Good News, and some to have the work
of caring for and teaching God's people.
Christ gave those gifts to prepare God's holy people
for the work of serving, to make the body of
Christ stronger.*

EPHESIANS 4:11–12 (NCV)

A LEADER'S PROMISE
TO THE TEAM

I WILL VALUE EVERYONE ON THIS TEAM
AND THEIR UNIQUE CONTRIBUTIONS TO THE
QUALITY AND ENJOYMENT OF OUR WORK.

BE CLEAR ABOUT ROLES

Where the word of a king is, there is power; and who may
say to him, "What are you doing?" He who keeps his command
will experience nothing harmful; And a wise man's heart
discerns both time and judgment . . .
All this I have seen, and applied my heart to every work
that is done under the sun: There is a time in
which one man rules over another to his own hurt.

ECCLESIASTES 8:4–5, 9

Solomon makes points about our relationship to the people who lead us. We are to submit to them, not because the person deserves it, but because the office deserves it and God decrees it. And what about leaders in authority? Solomon also issues a warning. When leaders try to exercise authority without a servant's heart, they eventually hurt themselves. Consider what he says.

ROLE OF THE FOLLOWER
1. Submit to God–given authority.
2. Trust God to accomplish His purpose.
3. Don't quit or become divisive.

ROLE OF THE LEADER
1. Exercise authority with wisdom and caution.
2. Recognize that no human controls all of life.
3. Lead others by serving, not bossing them.

The Maxwell Leadership Bible

CALL IN THE RESERVES

*After this the Lord appointed seventy–two others
and sent them two by two ahead of him to every town and
place where He was about to go.*

LUKE 10:1 (NIV)

If you look at the roster of any successful team, you will see that the starters are always outnumbered by the other players on the team. Teams that win championships have strong backups ready and waiting on the bench.

You find similar situations in every field. In the entertainment industry, the actors are often known, but the hundreds of necessary crew members aren't. For any politician or corporate executive or big–name fashion designer that you know about, hundreds of people are working quietly in the background to make their work possible. Nobody can neglect the majority of the team and hope to be successful.

Any team that wants to excel must have good substitutes as well as starters. You may be able to do some wonderful things with a handful of top people, but if you want your team to do well over the long haul, you've got to build your bench. A great team with no bench eventually collapses.

The 17 Indisputable Laws of Teamwork

Honor Everyone on the Team

*And those members of the body which we think
to be less honorable, on these we bestow greater honor . . .*

1 Corinthians 12:23

People who build successful teams never forget that every person's role is contributing to the bigger picture.

One of the best examples of this involves Winston Churchill. During World War II when Britain was experiencing its darkest days, the country had a difficult time keeping men working in the coal mines. Many wanted to give up their dirty, thankless jobs in the dangerous mines to join the military service, which got much public praise and support. Yet without coal, the military and the people at home would be in trouble.

So Churchill faced thousands of coal miners one day and passionately told them of their importance to the war effort, how their role could make or break the goal of maintaining England's freedom. It's said that tears appeared in the eyes of those hardened men. And they returned to their inglorious work with steely resolve. That's the kind of mindset it takes to build a team.

The 17 Indisputable Laws of Teamwork

THIS WEEK: Who are your starters? Your reserves? Does everyone know their role and their importance in it? Find a way to remind the reserves that they are appreciated and valued.

GOD'S PROMISE
TO LEADERS

Command those who are rich in this present age
not to be haughty, nor to trust in uncertain
riches but in the living God, who gives us richly
all things to enjoy. Let them do good,
that they be rich in good works, ready to give,
willing to share, storing up for themselves a good
foundation for the time to come,
that they may lay hold on eternal life.

1 TIMOTHY 6:17–19

A LEADER'S PROMISE
TO THE TEAM

I WILL TRAIN MYSELF TO BE GENEROUS
IN BOTH RELATIONSHIPS AND RESOURCES.

BE GENEROUS

If there is among you a poor man of your brethren,
within any of the gates in your land which the Lord your God
is giving you, you shall not harden your heart nor
shut your hand from your poor brother, but you shall open
your hand wide to him and willingly lend him
sufficient for his need, whatever he needs.

DEUTERONOMY 15:7–8

If great leaders err, they do so on the side of generosity. They are givers, not takers. They feel motivated to:

1. Serve others to help them grow and thrive.

2. Solve problems that prevent potential from being reached.

3. Save causes that benefit mankind.

God instructs His leaders and the entire nation of Israel to imitate His generosity and grace. At the end of every seventh year, every Israelite was to cancel all debts owed by fellow citizens. If they would indeed cancel debts, model graciousness and forgiveness, and care for the poor, God would favor their land with abundant crops and freedom from invasion. Imagine! They simply needed to trust that God was in control and let Him worry about rain and sun and fruitful harvest times.

The Maxwell Leadership Bible

Give Yourself Away

Speak up for the people who have no voice,
for the rights of all the down–and–outers. Speak out
for justice! Stand up for the poor and destitute!

Proverbs 31:8–9 (Msg)

Nothing has such a positive impact on a person as giving to others. That's because giving is the highest level of living. Generous people focus their time and energy on what they can give to others rather than what they can get from them. And the more a person gives, the better his attitude.

Most unsuccessful people don't understand this concept. They believe that how much people give and their attitude about it are based on how much they have. But it's not what you have that makes a difference. It's what you do with what you have. And that is based completely on attitude.

Sow a seed, change a life. It's been said that we make a living by what we get, but we make a life by what we give. Helping others is something you can start doing today, whether it's spending more time with your family, developing an employee who shows potential, helping people in the community, or putting your own desires on hold to benefit your team. The key is to find your purpose and help others while you're pursuing it. As entertainer Danny Thomas said: "All of us are born for a reason, but all of us don't discover why. Success in life has nothing to do with what you gain in life or accomplish for yourself. It's what you do for others."

Your Road Map for Success

Giving Is the Highest Level of Living

Then Abram gave him a tenth of everything.

Genesis 14:20 (NIV)

Nothing speaks to others more loudly than generosity from a leader. True generosity isn't an occasional event. It comes from the heart and permeates every aspect of a leader's life, touching their time, money, talents, and possessions. Effective leaders don't gather things just for themselves; they do it in order to give to others.

To cultivate the quality of generosity in your life, do the following:

1. Be grateful for whatever you have.
2. Put people first.
3. Don't allow the desire for possessions to control you.
4. See money as a resource.
5. Develop the habit of giving.

The only way to maintain an attitude of generosity is to make it your habit to give—your time, attention, money, and resources. As Richard Foster says, "Just the very act of letting go of money, or some other treasure, does something within us. It destroys the demon 'greed'."

The 21 Indispensable Qualities of a Leader

This Week: Consider what you're already giving, what you're being asked to give, and what you'd like to give even though you haven't been asked. Your reasons for accepting or denying requests might be good, but are they godly? How does it feel when you give?

GOD'S PROMISE
TO LEADERS

A light shines in the dark for honest people,
for those who are merciful and kind and good.
It is good to be merciful and generous.
Those who are fair in their business
will never be defeated.
Good people will always be remembered.

PSALM 112:4–6 (NCV)

A LEADER'S PROMISE
TO THE TEAM

I WILL MAKE OUR WORKPLACE AND OUR TEAM
INTERACTIONS AS POSITIVE AS POSSIBLE.
I WILL PRAISE THE GOOD IN OUR TEAM
EVEN WHEN WE MUST CONFRONT THE BAD.

WEEK 8

BE POSITIVE

I remind you to stir up the gift of God which is in you
through the laying on of my hands. For God has not given us
a spirit of fear, but of power and of love and of a sound mind.

2 TIMOTHY 1:6–7

People rise or fall to meet our level of expectations for them. If you express skepticism and doubt in others, they'll return your lack of confidence with mediocrity. But if you believe in them and expect them to do well, they'll wear themselves out trying to do their best. And in the process, both of you benefit.

If you've never been one to trust people and put your faith in them, change your way of thinking and begin believing in others. Your life will quickly begin to improve. When you have faith in another person, you give him or her an incredible gift, maybe the best gift you can give another person. Give others money, and it's soon spent. Give resources, and they may not be used to the greatest advantage. Give help, and they'll often find themselves back where they started in a short period of time. But give them your faith, and they become confident, energized, and self–reliant. They become motivated to acquire what they need to succeed on their own. And then later if you do share money, resources, and help, they're better able to use them to build a better future.

Becoming a Person of Influence

BOOSTING LOW MORALE

Nothing is more unpleasant than being on a team when nobody wants to be there. When that is the case, the team is usually negative, lethargic, or without hope. If you find yourself in that kind of situation, then do the following:

Investigate the situation. Address what the team is doing wrong and begin fixing what's broken.

Initiate belief. The only way for a team to change is if people believe in themselves. As the leader, you must initiate that belief.

Create energy. To bring a greater level of energy to the team, you need to be energetic. Eventually, your energy will spread.

Communicate hope. The greatest need of players at this stage is hope. Help them see the potential of the team.

To give the team a boost when morale is low, the leader must do productive things and pick up some speed. After all, you can't steer a parked car! To get the team moving . . .

Model behavior that has a high return. People do what people see.

Develop relationships with people of potential. Start with the people who have the potential to be productive. Remember, leaders touch a heart before they ask for a hand.

Set up small victories and talk teammates through them. Nothing helps people grow in skill and confidence like having some wins under their belts.

Communicate vision. Keep the vision before your team continually because vision gives team members direction and confidence.

The 17 Indisputable Laws of Teamwork

You're a 10!

I've never known a positive person yet who didn't love people and try to see the best in them. And one of the most effective ways to help you see the best in others is to do what I call putting a "10" on people's heads. Here's what I mean: We all have expectations of others, but we can choose whether those expectations are positive or negative. We can think that others are worthless or wonderful. When we make the decision to expect the best and actually look for the good instead of the bad, we're seeing them as a "10."

The ability to do this is important for a couple of reasons. First, we usually see in others what we expect to see. Second, people generally rise to meet our level of expectations.

Your Road Map for Success

THIS WEEK: The Pauline epistles are filled with instructions for growing in Christ, but Paul also made sure to encourage the young churches. Read Philippians 1:3–6 (NCV), and consider how you can similarly encourage your team members. "I thank my God every time I remember you, always praying with joy for all of you. I thank God for the help you gave me . . . God began doing a good work in you, and I am sure he will continue it until it is finished when Jesus Christ comes again."

GOD'S PROMISE
TO LEADERS

He who endures to the end shall be saved.

MATTHEW 24:13

A LEADER'S PROMISE
TO THE TEAM

WE WILL HAVE DIFFICULT TIMES,
BUT I WILL NOT LET THEM DETER US
FROM OUR GOALS. WE WILL ENDURE,
IMPROVE, AND OVERCOME.

BECOME A MOMENTUM MAKER

*And all Israel heard of the judgment which the king
had rendered; and they feared the king, for they saw that the
wisdom of God was in him to administer justice.*

1 KINGS 3:28

I t takes a leader to create momentum. Followers catch it. And managers are able to continue it once it has begun. But creating momentum requires someone who can motivate others, not someone who needs to be motivated. Just as every sailor knows you can't steer a ship that isn't moving forward, strong leaders understand that to change direction, you first have to create forward progress. Without momentum, even the simplest tasks can seem insurmountable. But with momentum on your side, nearly any kind of change is possible.

Consider the ways young Solomon created momentum:

• He started with what David provided.

• He made wise decisions that won him credibility.

• He maintained the peace.

No leader can ignore the impact of momentum. If you've got it, you and your people will be able to accomplish things you never thought possible. The choice to build momentum is yours.

The Maxwell Leadership Bible

DO THE LITTLE THINGS
TO MAINTAIN MOMENTUM

*These things I have spoken to you, that in Me
you may have peace. In the world you will have tribulation;
but be of good cheer, I have overcome the world.*

JOHN 16:33

When your people are winning and morale is high, you still have an important role as a leader. To help the team maintain high morale and momentum . . .

Keep the team focused and on course. If team members lose focus or get off course, then they'll stop winning.

Communicate successes. Nothing boosts morale like winning and then celebrating it.

Remove morale mashers. Once the team is rolling in the right direction, keep it rolling. Leaders see before others do, so they need to protect the team from the things that will hurt the team.

Allow other leaders to lead. When a leader prepares other team members to lead and then turns them loose to do it, two things result. First, it uses the existing momentum to create new leaders for the team. It's easier to make new leaders successful if they are part of a successful team. Second, it increases the leadership of the team. And that makes the team even more successful.

The process of building high morale is simple, but it isn't easy. It takes strong leadership, and it takes time.

The 17 Indisputable Laws of Teamwork

Go to the Very End

I have fought the good fight, I have finished the race,
I have kept the faith.

2 TIMOTHY 4:7

Even people who lack talent and fail to cultivate other vital qualities can contribute if they possess a tenacious spirit. Being tenacious means . . .

1. *Giving all that you have, not more than you have.* Some people mistakenly believe that being tenacious demands from them more than they have to offer. As a result, they don't push themselves. However, being tenacious requires that you give 100 percent—not more, but certainly not less.

2. *Working with determination, not waiting on destiny.* Tenacious people don't rely on luck, fate, or destiny for their success. They know that trying times are no time to quit trying.

3. *Quitting when the job is done, not when you're tired.* If you want your team to succeed, you have to keep pushing beyond what you think you can do. The victory isn't won until the last step in the relay race, the last shot in the basketball game, the last yard into the end zone.

The 17 Essential Qualities of a Team Player

THIS WEEK: Consider your track record of persistence and discipline. Where in your life and work do you need to improve? Read Hebrews 11 to review the list of some of the Bible's most amazing people of persistent faith. What could be said about you? "By faith, I, _____, persisted in _____."

GOD'S PROMISE
TO LEADERS

Fools will die because they refuse to listen;
they will be destroyed because they do not care.
But those who listen to [wisdom] will live in safety
and be at peace, without fear of injury."

PROVERBS 1:32–33 (NCV)

A LEADER'S PROMISE
TO THE TEAM

I RECOGNIZE THAT EVERYONE ON OUR TEAM
HAS INFLUENCE. YOUR INSIGHTS MATTER!
I WILL LISTEN TO YOU,
AND I WILL HELP YOU GROW.

BEGIN LEADING BY LOVING

A good leader motivates, doesn't mislead, doesn't exploit.

PROVERBS 16:10 (MSG)

If you desire to influence another person, the way to start is by nurturing them. What clergyman John Knox said over four hundred years ago is still true: "You cannot antagonize and influence at the same time."

At the heart of the nurturing process is genuine concern for others. And as we try to help and influence the people around us, we must have positive feelings and concern for them. If you want to help people and make a positive impact on them, you cannot dislike or disparage them. You must give love to them and give them respect.

You may be wondering why you should take on a nurturing role with the people you want to influence, especially if they are employees, colleagues, or friends. You may be saying to yourself, "Isn't that something they can get somewhere else, like at home?" The unfortunate truth is that most people are desperate for encouragement. If you become a major nurturer in the life of another person, then you have an opportunity to make a major impact on them.

Becoming a Person of Influence

UNEQUAL IN INFLUENCE

Influence is a curious thing. Even though we make some kind of impact on nearly everyone around us, we need to recognize that our level of influence is not the same with everyone. To see this principle in action, try ordering around your best friend's dog the next time you visit.

You may not have thought much about it, but you probably know instinctively which people you have great influence with and which ones you don't. One person may think all your ideas are great. Another may view everything you say with a great deal of skepticism. Yet that same skeptical person may love every single idea presented by your boss or one of your colleagues. That just shows your influence with him may not be as strong as that of someone else.

Becoming a Person of Influence

A position doesn't make a leader. A title may give someone authority, but not influence. Influence comes from the person; it must be earned. For instance, David was leading Israel long before Saul lost his throne (1 Chronicles 11:1–2). David had earned influence and Saul had not. Why was this so?

Unity. David rallied the people and created unity.

Identification. David identified with his followers as family.

Credibility. David effectively led military campaigns.

Anointing. David enjoyed God's hand and power on his life.

Partnership. David worked cooperatively with key leaders.

The Maxwell Leadership Bible

See the Leader, Know the Followers

People reflect their leader. We cannot expect followers to grow beyond their leader. We cannot expect followers to turn out fundamentally different from their leader. Consider what Proverbs 29 tells us about the influence of good and bad leaders:

Attitudes. When good leaders rule, people rejoice; when the wicked reign, people groan (v. 2).

Stability. When moral leaders rule, they establish justice; compromising leaders tear things down (v. 4).

Compassion. Good leaders express concern for the poor; bad leaders reflect no compassion for anyone (v. 7).

Honesty. When leaders pay attention to lies, their staff begins to esteem the same deceptions (v. 12).

Vision. Solid vision keeps everyone on track; chaos reigns wherever the vision lapses (v. 18).

The Maxwell Leadership Bible

This Week: Evaluate yourself according to the following formula: Competence + Character + Connection = Influence

How strong are you in each of those areas with regard to your work? Your family? Your community? Do you connect well with people? Do you exhibit excellence in your tasks? Is your character in line with your values? Do you see how all these elements cooperate to create your level of influence?

GOD'S PROMISE
TO LEADERS

Through Christ we feel certain before God. . . .
It is God who makes us able to do all that we do.

2 Corinthians 3:4–5 (NCV)

A LEADER'S PROMISE
TO THE TEAM

I'M CONFIDENT IN YOU,
AND I BELIEVE THAT TOGETHER
WE CAN ACCOMPLISH
WHAT WE NEED TO DO.

WEEK 11

BELIEVE IN YOURSELF

*"Let no man's heart fail because of him;
your servant will go and fight with this Philistine."*

1 SAMUEL 17:32

People will not follow a leader who does not have confidence in himself. In fact, people are naturally attracted to people who convey confidence.

An excellent example of this can be seen in an incident that occurred in Russia during an attempted coup. Army tanks surrounded the government building that housed President Boris Yeltsin and his pro–democracy supporters. As the army rolled into position, Yeltsin strode from the building, climbed up on a tank, looked the commander in the eye, and thanked him for coming over to the side of democracy. Later the commander admitted that although they had not intended to go over to his side, Yeltsin had appeared so confident that the soldiers decided to join him.

Confidence is a characteristic of a positive attitude. The greatest achievers remain confident regardless of circumstances. Strong leaders recognize and appreciate confidence in others. Confidence is not simply for show. Confidence empowers. Good leaders have the ability to instill within their people confidence in their own leadership. Great leaders have the ability to instill within their people confidence in themselves.

Developing the Leaders Around You

ARE PEOPLE DRAWN TO YOU?

Charisma is the ability to draw people to you. And like other character traits, it can be developed. Watch out for these roadblocks to charisma:

Pride. Nobody wants to follow a leader who thinks he is better than everyone else.

Insecurity. If you are uncomfortable with who you are, others will be too.

Moodiness. If people never know what to expect from you, they stop expecting anything.

Perfectionism. People respect the desire for excellence, but dread unrealistic expectations.

Cynicism. People don't want to be rained on by someone who sees a cloud around every silver lining.

If you can stay away from those qualities, you can cultivate charisma.

The 21 Indispensable Qualities of a Leader

Anointed to lead. When Moses brought the commandments, his face shone with the glory of God (Exodus 34:29). The Israelites perceived God's presence in Moses' leadership. Anointed leadership is characterized by:

1. *Charisma.* The anointed enjoy a sense of giftedness that comes from God. It seems magnetic.

2. *Character.* People see God's nature in your leadership. They trust you.

3. *Competence.* You have the ability to get the job done. Your leadership produces results.

4. *Conviction.* Your leadership has backbone. You always stand for what is right.

The Maxwell Leadership Bible

WHO YOU ARE IS WHO YOU ATTRACT

Then [Elisha] arose and followed Elijah,
and became his servant.

1 KINGS 19:21

Effective leaders are always on the lookout for good people. But who you get is not determined by what you want, but by who you are. In most situations, you draw people who possess the same qualities you do.

What enabled Elijah to draw like–minded people to his side? This truth: who you are is who you attract.

1. Every leader has a measure of magnetism.

2. A leader's magnetism may impact others intellectually, emotionally, or volitionally.

3. Magnetism is neither good nor bad in itself—it depends on what a leader does with it.

4. Secure leaders draw both similar and complementary followers.

5. A leader's magnetism never remains static.

It is possible for you to go out and recruit people unlike yourself, but it's crucial to recognize that people who are different will not naturally be attracted to you. Their quality depends on you. If you think the people you attract could be better, then it's time for you to improve yourself.

The Maxwell Leadership Bible

THIS WEEK: Consider how optimistic or pessimistic you are about yourself, your team, your current situation, and your mission. Who shares your mind? Who on your team is a positive influence on the others?

GOD'S PROMISE
TO LEADERS

My child, do not reject the LORD's discipline,
and don't get angry when he corrects you.
The LORD corrects those he loves,
just as parents correct the child they delight in.

PROVERBS 3:11–12 (NCV)

A LEADER'S PROMISE
TO THE TEAM

WHEN THERE'S A PROBLEM, I WILL DEAL WITH
IT DIRECTLY, PROMPTLY, AND RESPECTFULLY,
AND I WILL HELP US CORRECT
THE SITUATION TO GET BACK ON TRACK.

CARE ENOUGH TO CONFRONT

Then Nathan said to David, "You are the man!"

2 Samuel 12:7

Many people avoid confrontation. Some fear being disliked and rejected. Others are afraid confrontation will make things worse by creating anger and resentment in the person they confront. But avoiding confrontation always worsens the situation. Confrontation can be a win–win situation, a chance to help and develop your people– if you do it with respect and with the other person's best interests at heart. Here are ten guidelines to help you confront positively.

1. Confront ASAP.
2. Address the wrong action, not the person.
3. Confront only what the person can change.
4. Give the person the benefit of the doubt.
5. Be specific.
6. Avoid sarcasm.
7. Avoid words like "always" and "never."
8. If appropriate, tell the person how you feel about what was done wrong.
9. Give the person a game plan to fix the problem.
10. Affirm him or her as a person and a friend.

Positive confrontation is a sure sign that you care for a person and have their best interests at heart.

Developing the Leaders Around You

EVERYONE'S A CRITIC

Leaders can bank on two truths. First, they will be criticized. Second, criticism always changes the leader. Unhappy people tend to attack the point person. Notice what God and Moses teach us on how to handle criticism (Numbers 12).

1. Maintain your humility (v. 3).
2. Face the criticism squarely (v. 4).
3. Be specific about the issue (vv. 5–8).
4. Lay out consequences (vv. 9, 10).
5. Pray for the criticizers (vv. 12, 13).
6. Restore them when appropriate (v. 14).

Confrontation results in purity and security. Confrontation is not a punishment, but a redemptive act of leadership. The goals of healthy confrontation are . . .

Clarification. I will get a better understanding of the person and what happened.

Change. I hope to get improvement from it. And it may be me!

Relationship. I will likely deepen my relationship with this person.

Purity. As word gets out, the organization will be purified and sobered.

Respect. The organization will likely raise the members' level of respect for the leadership.

Security. People feel safe knowing leaders are strong enough to take a stand.

The Maxwell Leadership Bible

THE VELVET–COVERED BRICK

The apostle Paul loved his Corinthian brothers and sisters in Christ, but when he received reports that divisions, immorality, and pride had crept into the church, he knew he had to confront their sin (1 Corinthians 1:11). It was as if Paul were hitting them on the head with a velvet–covered brick—the brick being his condemnation of their sin, the velvet being his love for those whom God had set apart for good works. Paul practiced "The 101% Principle"—finding the 1 percent you can affirm, and giving it 100 percent of your attention. Remember, affirmation comes before confrontation. Good leaders look for the good in people and affirm it. Only then do they address the problems.

Paul's integrity also drove him to stand up to Peter, his fellow leader, in front of several Jewish and Gentile believers (Galatians 2:14). Consider his checklist for critiquing someone.

- Check your motive.
- Make sure the issue is worthy of criticism.
- Be specific.
- Don't undermine the person's self–confidence or identity.
- Do not postpone needed criticism.
- Look at yourself before looking at others.
- End criticism with encouragement.

The Maxwell Leadership Bible

THIS WEEK: Think about some recent or current conflicts. How promptly do you deal with conflicts? Are you good at confrontation? Review the checklists in this chapter several times before a confrontation. How did the confrontation go when you had the principles fresh in your mind?

GOD'S PROMISE
TO LEADERS

*When people are tempted and still
continue strong, they should be happy.
After they have proved their faith, God will
reward them with life forever.
God promised this to all those who love him.*

JAMES 1:12 (NCV)

A LEADER'S PROMISE
TO THE TEAM

I'M NOT PERFECT, BUT I KNOW WHO IS.
AND I'M DOING MY BEST TO BECOME MORE AND
MORE LIKE HIM IN BOTH MY PROFESSIONAL
LIFE AND IN MY PERSONAL LIFE.

WEEK 13

CHARACTER IS CRUCIAL

Live right, and you will eat from the life–giving tree.
And if you act wisely, others will follow.

<small>PROVERBS 11:30 (CEV)</small>

All leaders desire results, but being must precede doing.
• To achieve higher goals, you must be a more effective leader.

• To attract better people, you must be a better person yourself.

• To achieve greater results, you must be a person of great character.

A common problem occurs when a leader's real identity and the desired results don't match up. But when leaders display consistency of character, competence, and purpose, it makes a powerful statement to the people around them— and it draws those people to them.

If you desire to do great things with your life, then seek to become a better person and a better leader. Nothing great can be achieved alone. Any task worth doing requires the help of others. And if you want to attract good people, you've got to become a better person yourself. If you're willing to do that, then you can leave the results to God.

The 21 Most Powerful Minutes in a Leader's Day

COUNT ON CHARACTER

A thick bankroll is no help when life falls apart,
but a principled life can stand up to the worst.

PROVERBS 11:4 (MSG)

Crisis doesn't necessarily make character, but it certainly does reveal it. Adversity makes a person choose one of two paths: character or compromise. Every time leaders choose character, they become stronger even if that choice brings negative consequences. The development of character is at the heart of our development, not just as leaders, but as human beings.

What must every person know about character?

• Character is more than talk.

• Talent is a gift, but character is a choice.

• Character brings lasting success with people.

• Leaders cannot rise above the limitations of their character.

The 21 Indispensable Qualities of a Leader

Don't value talent above character. The enemy has targeted leaders for attack, and myriad leaders in the political, business, and religious worlds have fallen morally. Leaders need to remember that they influence many others beyond themselves; they never fall in a vacuum. We must take care not to emphasize the talents of a leader over his or her character. We have unhealthy tendency to see and reward the gift more than the character, but both are to be developed. We must strike the following balance if we are to finish well: Gift Deposited = Character Built.

The Maxwell Leadership Bible

GUARD YOUR THINKING

For as he thinks in his heart, so is he . . . Do not speak in the
hearing of a fool, for he will despise the wisdom of your words . . .
Apply your heart to instruction, and your ears to words
of knowledge . . . Do not let your heart envy sinners,
but be zealous for the fear of the LORD all the day; for surely
there is a hereafter, and your hope will not be cut off.
Hear, my son, and be wise; and guide your heart in the way.

PROVERBS 23:7, 9, 12, 17–19

Leaders understand the importance of their minds to the future of their organizations. Consider some of these timeless principles offered in Proverbs 23 about our minds and a godly vision for tomorrow.

• Your thoughts determine your character.

• Don't waste your thoughts on those who don't hunger for them.

• The first person you lead is you, and the first organ you master is your mind.

• Don't let your mind drift away from God's truth and into vain envy.

• Stay confident that your vision will come to pass.

• Discipline your thoughts to remain steadfast in what you know is right.

The Maxwell Leadership Bible

═══════════════════════

THIS WEEK: Consider the evidence of your character. Where is your character strong? Weak? Note how you respond in character–revealing and character–building situations this week.

GOD'S PROMISE
TO LEADERS

For the LORD gives wisdom;
From His mouth come knowledge and understanding;
He stores up sound wisdom for the upright;
He is a shield to those who walk uprightly;
He guards the paths of justice,
And preserves the way of His saints.
Then you will understand righteousness and justice,
Equity and every good path.

PROVERBS 2:6–9

A LEADER'S PROMISE
TO THE TEAM

AS I CHART THE COURSE FOR OUR TEAM,
I'M GUIDED BY THE TRUE NORTH STAR—
THE LORD—AND I'M EVALUATING OUR JOURNEY
ACCORDING TO HIS WISDOM.

CHART THE COURSE

The preparations of the heart belong to man,
But the answer of the tongue is from the LORD.
All the ways of a man are pure in his own eyes,
But the LORD weighs the spirits.
Commit your works to the LORD,
And your thoughts will be established.

PROVERBS 16:1–3

Effective leaders practice the Law of Navigation, which says that anyone can steer the ship, but it takes a leader to chart the course. The verses in Proverbs 16 remind leaders to:

- Check the source of their wisdom.
- Check their motives.
- Check the outcome they are pursuing.

Consider five key words to understanding how God helps leaders navigate their way through life:

Process. What is God revealing progressively?

Purpose. Why were you created?

Potential. God will use your gifts and passion. Does this goal fit who you are?

Prioritize. God will ask you to adjust your time and energy. What steps must you take?

Proceed. God will eventually require you to act. When should you start?

The Maxwell Leadership Bible

CHARTING YOUR OWN COURSE

As a good leader, Moses methodically arranged the tribal camps in the wilderness (Numbers 2:34). We would do well to plan and organize as he did.

• Give time for planning and organizing. Determine your primary purpose.

• Understand where you are before trying to develop a strategy.

• Prioritize the needs and goals of the team by asking the right questions.

• Write goals that are realistic, measurable, and convicting.

• Clarify goals and communicate with your team.

• Identify possible obstacles. Have an open system approach to your planning.

• Budget your cost and time by scheduling everything you can and setting deadlines.

• Study the results. Evaluation prevents stagnation and exaggeration.

Remember, anyone can steer the ship, but it takes a leader to chart the course.

The Maxwell Leadership Bible

Navigators do more than steer. They plan the whole trip in their minds before they leave the dock. They have a vision for their destination, they understand what it will take to get there, they know who they'll need on the team to be successful, and they recognize the obstacles long before they appear on the horizon. Leaders who prepare well can take their people just about anywhere.

The 21 Irrefutable Laws of Leadership

MOVING YOUR TEAM
IN THE RIGHT DIRECTION

Do you remember what it was like when you first got your driver's license? Just going for a drive was probably a thrill. It didn't really matter where you went. But as you got older, having a destination became more important. The same is true with a team.

Getting the team together and moving it are accomplishments, but where you're going matters. You've got to begin doing the difficult things that help the team to improve and develop high morale. Among other things, you must:

- Make changes that make the team better.
- Receive the buy–in of team members.
- Communicate commitment.
- Develop and equip members for success.

The two toughest stages in the life of a team are when you are trying to create movement in a team that's going nowhere, and when you must become a change agent. Those are the times when leadership is most needed.

The 17 Indisputable Laws of Leadership

THIS WEEK: Consider your team's journey. Is your team moving? Is it moving in the right direction? Does everyone know the destination? Is everyone aware of the challenges that await along the way? Is the morale of your team members an indicator of how prepared they are for the journey? Are you a good navigator?

GOD'S PROMISE
TO LEADERS

*In the past God spoke to our ancestors
through the prophets many times and in many
different ways. But now in these last days
God has spoken to us through his Son. God has
chosen his Son to own all things,
and through him he made the world.*

HEBREWS 1:1–2 (NCV)

A LEADER'S PROMISE
TO THE TEAM

IT IS IMPORTANT THAT WE UNDERSTAND
EACH OTHER. I WILL BE AS CLEAR,
CONSISTENT, AND COURTEOUS AS POSSIBLE IN
COMMUNICATING MY EXPECTATIONS,
INTENTIONS, CONCERNS, AND PRAISE.

COMMUNICATE TO LEAD

And so it was, when Jesus had ended these sayings,
that the people were astonished at His teaching, for He taught
them as one having authority, and not as the scribes.

MATTHEW 7:28–29

John W. Gardner observed, "If I had to name a single all–purpose instrument of leadership, it would be communication." If you cannot communicate, you will not lead others effectively. Give yourself three standards to live by as you communicate to your team.

Be consistent. Nothing frustrates team members more than leaders who can't make up their minds.

Be clear. Your team cannot execute if they don't know what you want. Don't try to dazzle anyone with your intelligence; impress them with your simple straightforwardness.

Be courteous. Everyone deserves to be shown respect, no matter what their position or what kind of history you might have with them. If you are courteous to your people, you set a tone for the entire organization.

Never forget that as the leader, your communication sets the tone for the interaction among your people.

The 17 Indisputable Laws of Teamwork

Make Communication Clear

The success of your marriage, job, and personal relationships all depend greatly on communication. You can be more a more effective communicator if you follow these four truths.

1. *Simplify your message.* Forget about impressing people with big words or complex sentences. If you want to connect with people, keep it simple.

2. *See the person.* As you communicate with individuals or groups, ask yourself these questions: Who is my audience? What are their questions? What needs to be accomplished?

3. *Show the truth.* Credibility precedes great communication. Believe in what you say. Then, live what you say. There is no greater credibility than conviction in action.

4. *Seek a response.* Never forget that the goal of all communication is action. Give people something to feel, something to remember, and something to do.

The 21 Indispensable Qualities of a Leader

Give yourself, not just your opinion. Note how communicators differ from public speakers.

Public Speaker	Communicator
1. Seeks to be understood and liked	1. Seeks to understand and connect
2. Asks: What do I have?	2. Asks: What do they need?
3. Focuses on techniques	3. Focuses on atmosphere
4. Is self–conscious	4. Is audience–oriented
5. Wants to complete the speech	5. Wants to complete the people
6. Is content–oriented	6. Is change–oriented

The Maxwell Leadership Bible

LEADERS TOUCH A HEART
BEFORE THEY ASK FOR A HAND

A leader can't connect with people only when he is communicating among groups; he must connect with individuals. The stronger the relationship and connection between individuals, the more likely the follower will help the leader. Successful leaders always initiate; they take the first step and make the effort to continue building relationships.

Connecting with people isn't complicated, but it takes effort. Observe the truths about connection that Rehoboam, son of David, ignored (1 Kings 12:16):

• Your people are more willing to take action when you first move them with emotion.

• When you give first, your people will give in return.

• When you connect with individuals, you gain the attention of crowds.

• When you reach out to your people, they will reach back toward you.

• Whether you have just taken over a leadership position or are well established, you must connect with your people if you are to succeed.

The Maxwell Leadership Bible

THIS WEEK: Consider the communication flow among your team members. Where does the information flow clearly and quickly? Where does information become muddied? As the chief communicator, do you connect well with your team?

GOD'S PROMISE
TO LEADERS

*Then Jesus said to his followers, "If people want
to follow me, they must give up the things
they want. They must be willing even to give up
their lives to follow me. . . . The Son of Man
will come again with his Father's glory
and with his angels. At that time,
he will reward them for what they have done."*

MATTHEW 16:24, 27 (NCV)

A LEADER'S PROMISE
TO THE TEAM

I'VE CONSIDERED THE COST OF THIS ENDEAVOR,
AND I COMMIT MYSELF TO FOLLOW THROUGH,
BECAUSE I BELIEVE WE WILL SEE REWARDS.

THE COST OF COMMITMENT

*Thus Hezekiah did throughout all Judah, and he did
what was good and right and true before the LORD his God.
And in every work that he began in the service of the
house of God, in the law and in the commandment, to seek
his God, he did it with all his heart. So he prospered.*

2 CHRONICLES 31:20–21

The Bible describes King Hezekiah as a leader who "did
what was good and right and true before the Lord his
God. And in every work that he began . . . he did it with
all his heart." Hezekiah paid the price to get the job done.
But what is the price of commitment?

1. *Change of lifestyle.* Hezekiah couldn't live the way his
father lived.

2. *Loneliness.* Hezekiah alone obeyed God at first.

3. *Faith in God.* Hezekiah believed that God would
bless his efforts.

4. *Criticism.* Hezekiah weathered the harsh questions
of an older generation.

5. *Hard work and money.* The king gave up time, energy,
and budget to reach his goal.

6. *Daily discipline.* Hezekiah had to instill a daily regimen
to bring about reform.

7. *Constant pressure.* The king endured the pressure of
potential failure and misunderstanding.

The Maxwell Leadership Bible

BE CAREFUL WHAT YOU PROMISE

*Do not be rash with your mouth, and let not your heart utter
anything hastily before God. For God is in heaven,
and you on earth; therefore let your words be few. . . .
When you make a vow to God, do not delay to pay it; for He
has no pleasure in fools. . . . Do not let your mouth cause
your flesh to sin, nor say before the messenger of God that it was
an error. Why should God be angry at your excuse and
destroy the work of your hands? For in the multitude of dreams
and many words there is also vanity. But fear God.*

ECCLESIASTES 5:2, 4, 6–7

Do you make promises to God? Scripture advises
caution before we commit something to God—good advice
for any decision a leader must make. Solomon describes
three major pitfalls lying in wait for careless leaders:

- *Hasty speech*. Leaders must listen as much as they speak.

- *Empty promises*. Leaders tend to say what others want
  to hear. Don't promise what you can't deliver.

- *Lame excuses*. Leaders diminish their influence when
  they try to reverse a mistake with a lame excuse.

The Maxwell Leadership Bible

Ask for commitment. Don't equip people who are
merely interested. Equip the ones who are committed.
Without commitment, there can be no success. To determine
whether your people are committed, make sure they know
what it will cost them. If they won't commit, don't go any
further in the equipping process. Don't waste your time.

Developing the Leaders Around You

THE COMMITMENT CRUCIBLE

Then Jesus said to the twelve, "Do you also want to go away?"
But Simon Peter answered Him, "Lord, to whom shall we go?
You have the words of eternal life."

JOHN 6:67–68

People often associate commitment with their emotions. If they feel the right way, then they can follow through on their commitments. But true commitment doesn't work that way. It's not an emotion; it's a character quality that enables us to reach our goals. Human emotions go up and down all the time, but commitment has to be rock solid.

There are some things every leader needs to know about being committed:

1. It usually is discovered amid adversity.
2. It does not depend on gifts or abilities.
3. It comes as the result of choice, not conditions.
4. It lasts when it's based on values.

The 17 Essential Qualities of a Team Player

THIS WEEK: Review the commitments pressing upon you. How did you prepare before accepting the commitments? Did you really know what you were getting into? What new commitments currently await your response? Who on your team is consistently good at accepting and following through on commitments? Who lets you down? Have you let down your team?

GOD'S PROMISE
TO LEADERS

But I will send you the Counselor—
the Spirit of truth. He will come to you from the
Father and will tell you all about me.
And you must also tell others about me because
you have been with me from the beginning.

JOHN 15:26–27 (NLT)

A LEADER'S PROMISE
TO THE TEAM

I WILL SEEK GOD AND GOOD ADVICE
FROM OTHERS AS I LEAD.

CREATE A STRONG INNER CIRCLE

Now these were the heads of the mighty men whom David had,
who strengthened themselves with him in his kingdom,
with all Israel, to make him king,
according to the word of the LORD concerning Israel.

1 CHRONICLES 11:10

There are no Lone Ranger leaders. If you're alone, you're not leading anybody. Examine the way King David pulled together the core people who made him great:

1. He built a strong inner circle before he needed it. David began building his team long before he was crowned king.

2. He attracted people with varied gifts. David attracted men of diverse abilities. We read of experienced warriors with a variety of skills, many men of valor, and hundreds of captains. With the help of these men, David felt ready for anything.

3. He engendered loyalty. David's followers displayed incredible loyalty to him throughout his life. Those closest to him seemed willing to put their lives on the line for him.

4. He delegated responsibility based on ability. David continually gave authority to others. He designated Joab as commander of the army, and he felt equally secure in giving others civil authority.

The Maxwell Leadership Bible

Some of David's first followers were misfits, yet he transformed his ragtag supporters into a winning team (1 Samuel 22:1–2). As David gained experience and grew in his leadership, he continued to attract stronger and stronger people. David made his inner circle great, and his inner circle made him great.

The 21 Most Powerful Minutes in a Leader's Day

No leader succeeds alone. Even David needed his Jonathan (1 Samuel 19:2–3). Do you have someone who "strengthens your hand in God"? All leaders need loyal friends who can help them persevere.

Choose your circle carefully. King Rehoboam had the benefit of his father's wise inner circle, but the foolish young king instead heeded advice that agreed with his own opinion (2 Chronicles 10:8). Horrible move! He should have gone with a core team with these qualities of a solid inner circle.

1. *Experience.* People who have been down the road of life and understand it.

2. *Heart for God.* People who place God first and uphold His values.

3. *Objectivity.* People who see the pros and cons of the issues.

4. *Love for people.* People who love others and value them more than things.

5. *Complementary gifts.* People who bring diverse gifts to the relationship.

6. *Loyalty to the leader.* People who truly love and are concerned for the leader.

The Maxwell Leadership Bible

BE FIRST TO TAKE YOUR GOOD ADVICE

My son, pay attention to my wisdom; Lend your ear to my understanding. That you may preserve discretion, And your lips may keep knowledge. For the lips of an immoral woman drip honey, And her mouth is smoother than oil; Remove your way far from her, And do not go near the door of her house, Lest you give your honor to others, And your years to the cruel one.

PROVERBS 5:1–3 & 8–9

It doesn't take a leader very long to realize that it's easier to give good advice than to follow it. Solomon proves the point. He tells us repeatedly and with great conviction that only fools fall into adultery. And yet, somehow, this same leader failed to heed God's explicit warning against kings taking many wives (Deuteronomy 17:17). Solomon blatantly disobeyed this command and married seven hundred women. The result? "His wives turned his heart after other gods; and his heart was not loyal to the Lord his God" (1 Kings 11:4).

Wise leaders not only give good advice; they heed it. How different the fortunes of Israel might have turned out had Solomon acted on the wisdom he so forcefully expressed to others!

The Maxwell Leadership Bible

THIS WEEK: Consider who sits in your inner circle. Do they share your vision? Do they have complementary gifts, useful where you need them most?

GOD'S PROMISE
TO LEADERS

*Then Jesus came to them and said, "All power in
heaven and on earth is given to me. So go and
make followers of all people in the world.
Baptize them in the name of the Father and the
Son and the Holy Spirit. Teach them to obey
everything that I have taught you, and I will be
with you always, even until the end of this age."*

MATTHEW 28:18–20 (NCV)

A LEADER'S PROMISE
TO THE TEAM

I TRUST YOU. I NEED YOU.
I WILL HELP YOU BECOME READY TO TAKE ON
MORE RESPONSIBILITIES, AND WHEN I DELEGATE
TO YOU I WILL MAKE SURE YOU HAVE THE
RESOURCES TO EXCEL IN YOUR TASKS.

DELEGATE TO TEAM MEMBERS

Abraham said to the oldest servant of his house . . . "Go to my country and to my family, and take a wife for my son Isaac."

GENESIS 24:2, 4

Delegation is the most powerful tool leaders have. Delegation increases individual productivity according to the number of people to whom leaders can delegate. It increases the productivity of their department or organization. Leaders who can't or won't delegate create a bottleneck to productivity. So why do some leaders fail to delegate effectively?

1. Insecurity
2. Lack of confidence in others
3. Lack of ability to train others
4. Personal enjoyment of the task
5. Habit
6. Inability to find someone else to do it
7. Lack of time
8. An "I do it best" mind–set

If you recognize yourself in any of the issues above, you probably aren't doing enough delegating. Here are some other indicators that you need to delegate: When deadlines are missed often; crises become frequent; someone else could do the job; or those under your leadership need another world to conquer.

Developing the Leaders Around You

DECIDE TO DELEGATE

One of the most common mistakes a coach can make is to misjudge the level of a player. If the leader doesn't work with each player according to where he is in his development, the player won't produce, succeed, and develop. According to management consultant Ken Blanchard, all team members fit into one of four categories with regard to the type of leadership they need:

Players who need direction. These players don't know what to do or how to do it. You need to instruct them every step of the way.

Players who need coaching. Players who are able to do more of the job on their own will become more independent, but they still rely on you for direction and feedback.

Players who need support. Players able to work without your direction still may require resources and encouragement.

Players to whom you delegate. When these players are given a task, you can be confident that it will be done. They only need you to lead. Provide them with vision on the front end and accountability on the back end, and they will multiply your efforts toward success.

Developing the Leaders Around You

It takes a team. God's answer to Moses' cry for help was for Moses to share the responsibilities of leadership with a select group (Numbers 11:14). When a leader called by God has a burden that becomes too great, God provides help . . . if the leader will ask for it. He also will anoint them with His power, just as He did the seventy elders of Israel.

The Maxwell Leadership Bible

SHARE THE BURDEN

Moreover you shall select from all the people able men . . .
And let them judge the people at all times. Then it will be that
every great matter they shall bring to you, but every small
matter they themselves shall judge. So it will be easier for you,
for they will bear the burden with you.

EXODUS 18:21–22

Easing people into delegation is important. You can't simply dump tasks on people, not if you want them to succeed. Delegate according to the following steps:

1. Ask them to be fact finders only. It gives them a chance to become acquainted with the issues and objectives.

2. Ask them to make suggestions. This gets them thinking and it gives you a chance to become acquainted with their thought processes.

3. Ask them to implement one of their recommendations, but only after you give your approval. Set them up for success, not failure.

4. Ask them to take action on their own, but to report the results immediately. This will give them confidence, and you will still be able to perform damage control if necessary.

5. Give complete authority. This is what you've been working toward.

Developing the Leaders Around You

THIS WEEK: Consider some specific tasks that you and/or your team must do. Per task, is the responsible person someone who needs direction, coaching, support, or delegation?

GOD'S PROMISE
TO LEADERS

Each one of us did the work God gave us to do.
I planted the seed, and Apollos watered it.
But God is the One who made it grow. . . .
The one who plants and the one who waters have
the same purpose, and each will be
rewarded for his own work.

1 CORINTHIANS 3:5–6, 8 (NCV)

A LEADER'S PROMISE
TO THE TEAM

I CANNOT FULFILL OUR MISSION ALONE.
I WANT TO EMPOWER YOU.
I INVITE YOU TO SHARE YOUR DESIRE TO GROW,
SO WE CAN MAKE IT HAPPEN TOGETHER.

EMPOWER YOUR PEOPLE

I want to share a secret with you. It's the greatest principle I've ever learned in the area of developing others. Here it is: Never work alone. I know that sounds too simple, but it is truly the secret to developing others. Whenever you do anything that you want to pass along to others, take someone along with you.

This isn't necessarily a natural practice for many of us. The most common learning model in the United States is when a leader asks questions or lectures while the follower listens and tries to comprehend the instructor's ideas. But craftsmen use a different model for developing others. They take apprentices who work alongside them until they master their craft and are able to pass it along to others. Their model looks something like this:

I do it.

I do it—and you watch.

You do it—and I watch.

You do it.

In all the years I've been equipping and developing others, I've never found a better way to do it than this.

Your Road Map for Success

Evaluate, Then Empower

If anyone wants to provide leadership in the church, good!
But there are preconditions.

1 Timothy 3:1 (Msg)

The way to start empowering people is by evaluating them. With inexperienced people, if you give them too much authority too soon, you can be setting them up to fail. With people who have lots of experience, if you move too slowly you can frustrate and demoralize them.

Remember that everyone has the potential to succeed. Your job is to see the potential, find out what he lacks, and equip him with what he needs. As you evaluate the people you intend to empower, look first at three areas:

1. *Knowledge.* Think about what people need to know in order to do anything you intend to give them.

2. *Skill.* Nothing is more frustrating than being asked to do things for which you have no ability.

3. *Desire.* No amount of skill, knowledge, or potential can help a person succeed if he doesn't have the desire to be successful.

Becoming a Person of Influence

Invest to empower. To be an empowering leader, you must do more than believe in emerging leaders. You need to take steps to help them become the leaders they have the potential to be. Empowering people takes a personal investment. It requires energy and time. But it's worth the price. And when you empower others, you create power in your organization.

The Maxwell Leadership Bible

THE POWER TO CHANGE THE WORLD

All the training in the world will provide only limited success if you don't turn your people loose to do the job. The way to do that is to give them responsibility, authority, accountability, and resources.

Responsibility may seem like the easiest to give, but some leaders find it difficult to allow their people to keep the responsibility after it's been given. Poor managers want to control every detail of their people's work. When that happens, the potential leaders who work for them become frustrated and don't develop. Rather than desiring more responsibility, they become indifferent or avoid responsibility altogether.

With responsibility must go authority. Winston Churchill said, "I am your servant. You have the right to dismiss me when you please. What you have no right to do is ask me to bear responsibility without the power of action."

Once responsibility and authority have been given to people, they become empowered to make things happen. But we also have to be sure that they are accountable for making the right things happen.

Resources are necessary for fulfilling responsibilities. This includes much more than just equipment. It includes training and professional development. Be willing to spend money on books, tapes, conferences, and the like. Be creative in providing tools. It will keep your people growing and equip them to do the job well.

Developing the Leaders Around You

THIS WEEK: Reflect on your own journey. Who empowered you along the way? How can you be more deliberate in empowering your team?

GOD'S PROMISE
TO LEADERS

Be of good courage,
And He shall strengthen your heart,
All you who hope in the LORD.

PSALM 31:24

A LEADER'S PROMISE
TO THE TEAM

I WILL BE AN ENLARGER. I WILL ENCOURAGE
THE BEST QUALITIES IN INDIVIDUALS
AND IN THE TEAM AS A WHOLE.

ENLARGE YOUR PEOPLE

Good leadership is a channel of water controlled by GOD;
he directs it to whatever ends he chooses.

PROVERBS 21:1 (MSG)

With good leadership, everything improves. Leaders are lifters. They push the thinking of their teammates beyond old boundaries of creativity. They elevate others' performance, making them better than they've ever been. They improve people's confidence in themselves and others. While managers are often able to maintain a team at its current level, leaders are able to lift it to a higher level than it has ever reached before. The key to that is working with people and bringing out the best in them. For example:

Leaders transfer ownership for work to those who execute the work.

Leaders create an environment where each team member wants to be responsible.

Leaders coach the development of personal capabilities.

Leaders learn quickly and encourage others to learn efficiently also.

If you want to give a team a lift, then provide it with better leadership.

The 17 Indisputable Laws of Teamwork

GIVE THEM THEMSELVES

Team members always love and admire a person who is able to help them go to another level, someone who enlarges them and empowers them to be successful. Players who enlarge their teammates have several things in common.

1. Enlargers value their teammates. People's performances usually reflect the expectations of those they respect.

2. Enlargers know and relate to what their teammates value. Players who enlarge others understand what their teammates value. That kind of knowledge, along with a desire to relate to their fellow players, creates a strong connection between teammates.

3. Enlargers add value to their teammates. An enlarger looks for the gifts, talents, and uniqueness in other people, and then helps them increase those abilities for their benefit and for that of the entire team.

4. Enlargers make themselves more valuable. You cannot give what you do not have. If you want to increase the ability of a teammate, make yourself better.

The 17 Essential Qualities of a Team Player

When people are esteemed, relationships are redeemed. Leaders know that people are an organization's most appreciable asset; therefore, people skills are a leader's most important attribute. Proverbs 27 presents some fundamentals on relationships.

1. Don't brag.
2. Don't envy.
3. Be forthright.
4. Don't forsake your roots.
5. Stay close.
6. Add value.
7. Don't be moved by flattery.

The Maxwell Leadership Bible

BLESSED FOR SUCCESS

And he blessed Joseph, and said, " . . . The Angel who has
redeemed me from all evil, bless the lads;
Let my name be named upon them, and the name
of my fathers Abraham and Isaac; and let them grow into
a multitude in the midst of the earth."

GENESIS 48:15–16

Not everyone you influence will think the same way you do. You have to help them not only believe that they can succeed, but also show them that you want them to succeed. How do you do that?

Expect it. People can sense your underlying attitude no matter what you say or do. If you have an expectation for your people to be successful, they will know it.

Verbalize it. People need to hear you tell them that you believe in them and want them to succeed. Become a positive prophet of their success.

Reinforce it. You can never do too much when it comes to believing in people.

Once people recognize and understand that you genuinely want to see them succeed and are committed to helping them, they will begin to believe they can accomplish what you give them to do.

Becoming a Person of Influence

THIS WEEK: Make a point to enlarge everyone on your team. Note how they react—both immediately and in the successive hours and days. How can you enlarge people on a more consistent basis?

GOD'S PROMISE
TO LEADERS

We know that in everything God works for the good of those who love him. They are the people he called, because that was his plan.

Romans 8:28 (NCV)

A LEADER'S PROMISE
TO THE TEAM

When I fail,
I will accept responsibility,
learn from my mistakes,
and get back in the game.

FAIL FORWARD

Have mercy upon me, O God,
According to Your lovingkindness;
According to the multitude of Your tender mercies,
Blot out my transgressions.
Wash me thoroughly from my iniquity,
And cleanse me from my sin.
For I acknowledge my transgressions,
And my sin is always before me . . .
Create in me a clean heart, O God,
And renew a steadfast spirit within me.

PSALM 51:1–3, 10

Mistakes are a part of life. Successful leaders recognize their errors, learn from them, and then work to correct their faults. A study of 105 executives determined many of the characteristics of successful executives, but one particular trait they shared was identified as the most valuable. It was that they admitted their mistakes and accepted the consequences rather than trying to blame others.

Most people don't want to reap the consequences of their actions. You can see this type of attitude everywhere. A leader who is willing to take responsibility for their actions and be honest or "transparent" with their people is someone they will admire, respect, and trust. That leader is also someone they can learn from.

Developing the Leaders Around You

ACCEPT RESPONSIBILITY
AND GET BACK IN THE GAME

When things go wrong, the natural tendency is to look for someone to blame. You can go all the way back to the Garden of Eden on this one. When God asked Adam what he'd done, he said it was Eve's fault. Then when God questioned Eve, she blamed it on the snake. The same thing happens today.

The next time you experience a failure, think about why you failed instead of who was at fault. Try to look at it objectively so that you can do better next time. Ask yourself:

What lessons have I learned?

How can I turn the failure into success?

Where did I succeed as well as fail?

People who blame others for their failures never overcome them. They simply move from problem to problem. To reach your potential, you must continually improve yourself, and you can't do that if you don't take responsibility for your actions and learn from your mistakes.

In life, you will have problems. Are you going to give up and stay down, wallowing in your defeat, or are you going to get back on your feet as quickly as you can?

When you fall, make the best of it and get back on your feet. Learn what you can from your mistake, and then get back in the game. View your errors the way Henry Ford did his. He said, "Failure is the opportunity to begin again more intelligently."

Your Road Map for Success

Don't Take Yourself Too Seriously

A merry heart does good, like medicine.

Proverbs 17:22

I work with a lot of leaders. And one thing I've found is that many times they take themselves much too seriously. Of course, they're not alone. I meet people in every walk of life who have too much doom and gloom in their attitudes. They simply need to lighten up. No matter how serious your work is, that's no reason to take yourself seriously.

If any person had a reason to take his job and himself seriously, it would be a president of the United States. Yet it's possible for even people holding that position to maintain their sense of humor and keep their egos in check. For example, when Calvin Coolidge was asked if he was attending the Sesquicentennial Exposition in Philadelphia, the president answered, "Yes."

"Why are you going, Mr. President?" a reporter asked.

"As an exhibit," answered the rotund Coolidge.

If you tend to take yourself too seriously, give yourself and everyone else around you a break. Recognize that laughter breeds resilience. Laughing is the quickest way to get up and get going again when you've been knocked down.

Failing Forward

This Week: Think about your recent failures at work and at home. What have you learned from those experiences? Did you take your share of responsibility? Did you blame others unduly? How can you begin again more intelligently? Can you laugh at yourself?

GOD'S PROMISE
TO LEADERS

It is my family God has chosen!
Yes, he has made an everlasting covenant with me.
His agreement is eternal, final, sealed.
He will constantly look after my safety and success.

2 SAMUEL 23:5 (NLT)

A LEADER'S PROMISE
TO THE TEAM

MY FAMILY COMES FIRST, AND BECAUSE I DO
A GOOD JOB LEADING THE PEOPLE WHO MEAN
THE MOST TO ME, YOU CAN TRUST ME
TO TAKE SIMILAR CARE IN LEADING THIS TEAM.

FAMILY FIRST

*But if anyone does not provide for his own,
and especially for those of his household, he has denied the faith
and is worse than an unbeliever.*

1 TIMOTHY 5:8

Every day parents and spouses leave their families in the pursuit of success. It's almost as though they're driving down the road, and they get pretty far along before they realize they've left members of their family behind. The tragedy is that many value their careers, success, or personal happiness more than they do their families. They decide that it's too much work to go back, so they just keep driving.

But what many are now realizing is that the hope of happiness at the expense of breaking up a family is an illusion. You can't give up your marriage or neglect your children and gain true success.

To build a strong family, you have to make your home a supportive environment. Psychologist William James said, "In every person from the cradle to the grave, there is a deep craving to be appreciated." Feeling appreciated brings out the best in people. And when that appreciation comes in the home and is coupled with acceptance, love, and encouragement, the bonds between family members grow, and the home becomes a safe haven for everyone.

Your Road Map for Success

LEADERSHIP BEGINS AT HOME

As a leader, where should your influence begin? A good answer can be drawn from the life of Joshua. To him, leading his family was more important than leading his country (Joshua 24:15). It may sound ironic, but when leaders put their families first, the community benefits. When leaders put the community first, both their families and the community suffer. Starting at home is always the key to affecting others in a positive way. Because Joshua had his priorities right and had led his household well, he gained credibility to lead the entire house of Israel.

If you have a family, put them first in your leadership. There's no legacy like that of the positive influence leaders can exercise with their family.

The 21 Most Powerful Minutes in a Leader's Day

Lead your children well. Eli's failure to lead his family eventually led to his downfall as a religious leader (1 Samuel 2:22–36). He lost his credibility, his job, and eventually his life. He missed the mark by making some crucial errors.

1. *Emphasis.* Eli emphasized teaching his colleagues and clients, not his family.

2. *Expectations.* Eli thought his sons would "get it" just because they lived in the house of the Lord.

3. *Example.* Eli failed to live out in his home what he taught in his work.

4. *Entanglements.* Eli got so caught up with his profession, he blinded himself to his failure.

The Maxwell Leadership Bible

LEADERSHIP IS MORE EXAMPLE THAN POWER

Leadership in the home is not about power or control; it's about giving up yourself for someone else. Evaluate your home leadership in each of the following categories:

Initiative. Do I give direction and take responsibility for my primary relationships?

Intimacy. Do I experience intimacy with God and others through open conversations?

Influence. Do I exercise biblical influence by encouraging and developing others?

Integrity. Do I lead an honest life?

Identity. Am I secure in who I am?

Inner circle. Do I exhibit the fruit of the Spirit in my life, including self-discipline?

"Train up a child in the way he should go, and when he is old he will not depart from it" (Proverbs 22:6). God calls parents to lead their children, and focusing on three key words can help.

Modeling. A good example is worth a thousand sermons.

Management. Good management is the ability to discern the uniqueness of a child and teach him or her accordingly.

Memories. The verse says, "When he is old, he will not depart . . ." This implies that the child has special memories of his early experiences.

The Maxwell Leadership Bible

THIS WEEK: Evaluate the leadership in your home. Are you giving your best to the people you love? Are you modeling what you want your family to do, too? What were the leaders like where you grew up? How is that modeling experience affecting you today as a leader?

GOD'S PROMISE
TO LEADERS

The humble He guides in justice,
And the humble He teaches His way.
All the paths of the LORD are mercy and truth,
To such as keep His covenant and His testimonies.

PSALM 25:9–10

A LEADER'S PROMISE
TO THE TEAM

AS I LEAD YOU, I AM ALSO ENDEAVORING
TO LEARN AND GROW AS A LEADER MYSELF.

FIND A MENTOR

*Then Moses spoke to the LORD, saying: "Let the LORD . . .
set a man over the congregation . . . that the congregation of the
LORD may not be like sheep which have no shepherd."
And the LORD said to Moses: "Take Joshua the
son of Nun with you, a man in whom is the Spirit."*

NUMBERS 27:15–18

Joshua was an impressive leader. One of the major factors in Joshua's increase in influence was the impact of Moses on his life. Wherever Moses went, Joshua went with him, whether it was up Mount Sinai or to meet with God in the tabernacle.

After the Hebrews refused to enter the Promised Land, the mentoring relationship between the two men continued. In fact, the process continued for forty years and culminated with Moses imparting his authority to the younger man. And after Moses died, no one questioned Joshua's leadership.

Pastor A. W. Tozer said, "God is looking for people through whom He can do the impossible—what a pity that we plan only the things we can do by ourselves." Moses' investment in Joshua released God's power in him.

The 21 Most Powerful Minutes in a Leader's Day

Choosing a Leadership Model

Give great thought to which leaders you follow because they determine your course as a leader. Here are six questions to consider before picking a model to follow.

1. Does my model's life deserve a following?
2. Does my model's life already have a following?
3. What is the main strength that influences others to follow my model?
4. Does my model reproduce other leaders?
5. Is my model's strength reproducible in my life?
6. If my model's strength is reproducible in my life, what steps must I take to develop and demonstrate that strength?

Remember, studying national or historical figures can certainly benefit you, but not the way a personal mentor can.

Be a worthy follower. Use these guidelines to help develop a positive mentoring relationship.

Ask the right questions. Make the questions strategic for your growth.

Don't let ego get in the way of learning.

Respect mentors but don't idolize them.

Put into effect immediately what you are learning.

Be disciplined in relating to mentors. Arrange for ample time, select the subject matter in advance, and do your homework.

Don't threaten to give up. Let mentors know they're not wasting their time.

Developing the Leaders Around You

Choose Your Mentor Well

Every leader needs mentors, especially emerging leaders. God took Elisha through the preparation necessary under Elijah. Note several principles outlined in 1 Kings 19 and 2 Kings 2 underlying his preparation:

Elisha's Preparation	Leadership Principle
1. He was anointed to replace Elijah.	1. Leaders must understand their call and role.
2. Elisha touched Elijah's mantle long before he entered his ministry.	2. Leaders must wait patiently on God's perfect timing for their authority.
3. Elisha burned his farming tools.	3. Leaders must surrender former ambitions.
4. Elisha stuck with Elijah wherever he went.	4. Leaders must pursue good mentors.
5. Elisha absorbed all he could from Elijah.	5. Leaders must hunger to grow and develop.

The Maxwell Leadership Bible

***

THIS WEEK: Consider how God is mentoring you. Who and what has He used to grow you in faith? In servant leadership? What do you hunger to learn? Can you think of other leaders who might be good mentors for you? Will you ask them to teach you?

GOD'S PROMISE
TO LEADERS

When people's steps follow the LORD,
God is pleased with their ways.
If they stumble, they will not fall,
because the LORD holds their hand.

PSALM 37:23–24 (NCV)

A LEADER'S PROMISE
TO THE TEAM

I KNOW WHO MY LEADER IS,
AND I'M ALERT TO HIS CALL.

FOLLOW THE ULTIMATE LEADER

Then God said, "Let us make man in our image, in our likeness, and let them rule over the fish of the sea and the birds of the air, over the livestock, over all the earth . . ."

GENESIS 1:26 (NIV)

God is the Ultimate Leader, and He calls every believer to lead others. God could have arranged His creation in any number of ways, but He chose to create human beings who possess spirits and the capacity to relate to Him and follow Him, yet who are not forced to do so.

When mankind fell into sin, God could have executed a plan of redemption that did not include sinful people, but He has called us to participate and to lead others as we follow Him. God made that clear from the beginning when He stated, "have dominion" (Genesis 1:28).

The call to leadership is a consistent pattern in the Bible. When God decided to raise up a nation of His own, He didn't call upon the masses. He called out one leader—Abraham. When He wanted to deliver His people out of Egypt, He didn't guide them as a group. He raised up a leader to do it—Moses. When it came time for the people to cross into the Promised Land, they followed one man—Joshua.

Every time God desired to do something great, He called a leader to step forward. Today He still calls leaders to step forward for every work, both large and small.

The Maxwell Leadership Bible

FIRE OF GOD

"Who among us shall dwell with the devouring fire?
Who among us shall dwell with everlasting burnings?"
He who walks righteously and speaks uprightly, he who despises
the gain of oppressions, who gestures with his hands,
refusing bribes, who stops his ears from hearing of bloodshed,
and shuts his eyes from seeing evil.

ISAIAH 33:14–15

Isaiah lays out a list of traits for the kind of people who can stand up in a crisis. Ponder his description:

Integrity. The leader's life and words match.

Justice. The leader rejects dishonest gain.

Convictions. The leader's values won't allow him or her to accept bribes.

Positive focus. The leader rejects destructive thinking.

Pure. The leader disciplines his or her mind to remain clean and pure.

Secure. The leader is firm, stable in his or her identity and source of strength.

Calling all leaders! When the Lord wanted someone to speak to the people for Him, Isaiah answered the call (Isaiah 6) because of three factors that still call leaders today.

Opportunity. We see a specific place where we can make a difference. This has to do with timing.

Ability. We recognize that we have the God–given gifts to do something about the need. This has to do with competence.

Desire. We want to step out and address the need; our hunger pushes us. This has to do with passion.

The Maxwell Leadership Bible

FOLLOW MY LEAD

Look at every phase of Joshua's life, and you see a man who gave himself wholeheartedly to completing whatever task was assigned to him. From the first, he immediately obeyed the instruction of Moses (Exodus 17:9–10). Thereafter Joshua took on the role of Moses' assistant. Joshua again displayed his obedience when he agreed to spy out the Promised Land. Upon his return from the reconnaissance mission, he and Caleb, alone among the spies, were ready to obey God and enter Canaan. Forty years later when Moses handed the reins of power to his protégé, Joshua again obeyed the call (Joshua 1:5–11).

In the end, the people of Israel followed Joshua's example and did what God asked of them—and as a result inherited the land God had promised.

By the time of his death, Joshua was known simply as "the servant of the Lord" (Judges 2:7–8). That is high praise! While today we consider Joshua an exceptional leader, nowhere does Scripture describe him as a man of extraordinary might, intellect, or talent. Obedience made him extraordinary. And when you're a servant of the Lord, that's all you really need.

The Maxwell Leadership Bible

THIS WEEK: Consider your call to leadership. How were you called? Can you see God's hand in your preparation? How have you been refined along the way? Is your call the same today as it was in the beginning? How has it changed? Is it changing now?

GOD'S PROMISE
TO LEADERS

*For the kingdom of God is . . . righteousness
and peace and joy in the Holy Spirit. For he who
serves Christ in these things is acceptable
to God and approved by men.*

ROMANS 14:17–18

A LEADER'S PROMISE
TO THE TEAM

I'M HERE TO SERVE THIS TEAM
SO TOGETHER WE CAN FULFILL OUR PURPOSE.

GIVE YOURSELF AWAY

But whoever desires to become great among you,
let him be your servant. And whoever desires to be first
among you, let him be your slave.

MATTHEW 20:26–27

As a team leader, how do you cultivate an attitude of selflessness among your people? Begin this way:

1. *Being generous.* Saint Francis of Assisi said, "All getting separates you from others; all giving unites you to others." If team members are willing to give of themselves generously to the team, then it is being set up to succeed.

2. *Avoiding internal politics.* One of the worst forms of selfishness can be seen in people who are playing politics on the team. That usually means posturing or positioning themselves for their own benefit, regardless of how it might damage the team. But good team players worry about the benefit of their teammates more than themselves.

3. *Displaying loyalty.* If you show the people on your team loyalty, they will return loyalty in kind. Loyalty fosters unity, and unity breeds team success.

4. *Valuing interdependence more than independence.* In the United States, we value independence highly, because it is often accompanied by innovation, hard work, and a willingness to stand for what's right. But independence taken too far is a characteristic of selfishness.

LET GOD WORRY ABOUT YOUR PROMOTION

Don't work yourself into the spotlight;
Don't push your way into the place of prominence.
It's better to be promoted to a place of honor
Than face humiliation by being demoted.

PROVERBS 25:6–7 (MSG)

In his first letter to Timothy, the apostle Paul tells us that aspiring to a position of leadership is a good thing (3:1). However, there's a difference between stepping forward to accept the responsibility of leadership and stepping forward to put yourself into the spotlight for the benefit of self–promotion.

The road to biblical leadership comes through service. Leaders may find themselves in the spotlight, but they also take the heat that often comes with that place of prominence. They speak up for the sake of the mission, but they are also willing to remain silent when it serves the organization. And at any moment, they must be willing to make all kinds of sacrifices for the sake of their people.

Leaders lose the right to be selfish. Romans 15:1–6 reminds us that leadership is about serving others, not wielding power. A servant . . .

1. denies self. We are to please others, not ourselves.
2. develops others. We are to add value to others.
3. accepts mistreatment. We are to forgive wrongs.
4. imitates Christ. We are to look to Jesus as our model.
5. is a student. We are to remain teachable.
6. pursues the harmony of relationships. We are to pursue unity and peace.

The Maxwell Leadership Bible

OH, IT'S NOTHING

*Then news of these things came to the ears of the church
in Jerusalem, and they sent out Barnabas to go as far as
Antioch. When he came and had seen the grace of God, he
was glad, and encouraged them all that with purpose of
heart they should continue with the Lord. For he was a
good man, full of the Holy Spirit and of faith. And a
great many people were added to the Lord.*

ACTS 11:22–24

If any early church leader could be called a servant, it
is Barnabas. He initiated and did whatever it took to raise
morale, men, or money. What allowed Barnabas to
demonstrate such a lifestyle? He had . . .

Nothing to prove. Barnabas didn't have to play games.
He never sought the limelight. When he mentored Paul,
he happily let the emerging apostle rise above him.

Nothing to lose. Barnabas didn't have to guard his
reputation or fear that he would lose popularity. He came to
serve, not to be served. This enabled him to focus on giving,
not getting.

Nothing to hide. Barnabas didn't maintain a facade or
image. He remained authentic, vulnerable, and transparent.
He could rejoice with other's victories.

The Maxwell Leadership Bible

THIS WEEK: In what ways are you an effective servant of
your team? In what ways do you struggle? Seek out an
opportunity to quietly serve someone on your team, and
take note of the results.

GOD'S PROMISE
TO LEADERS

A man's heart plans his way,
But the LORD directs his steps. . . .
He who heeds the word wisely will find good,
And whoever trusts in the LORD, happy is he.

PROVERBS 16:9, 20

A LEADER'S PROMISE
TO THE TEAM

ALTHOUGH I VALUE EVERYONE'S OPINION,
I WILL GIVE EXTRA CONSIDERATION TO THOSE
WHO HAVE PROVEN THEMSELVES TO BE WISE,
RELIABLE, AND COMMITTED TO THE
WELLBEING OF OUR TEAM AND OUR MISSION.

GOOD ADVICE
CAN MAKE YOU GREAT

Blessed is the man who walks not in the counsel of the ungodly,
nor stands in the path of sinners, nor sits in the seat
of the scornful; But his delight is in the law of the Lord,
and in His law he meditates day and night. He shall be like a
tree planted by the rivers of water, that brings forth its fruit
in its season, whose leaf also shall not wither;
And whatever he does shall prosper.

PSALM 1:1–3

The brilliant first psalm contrasts the righteous and the wicked. Leaders, take note, because the difference between the two seems to be where they get their counsel! Observe how a foolish leader can be led astray by a corrupt inner circle.

1. The leader begins to browse for the wrong counsel.
2. The leader begins to listen to the wrong voices.
3. The leader joins the wrong inner circle.

A wise leader meditates on God's Word day and night. Note the results of receiving counsel from the right inner circle.

1. Stability
2. Inward nourishment and refreshment
3. Fruitfulness and productivity
4. Strength and durability
5. Success

The Maxwell Leadership Bible

Your Advisors Will Make or Break You

Every leader ought to build an inner circle that adds value to him or her and to the leadership of the organization. But choose well, for the members of this inner circle will become your closest confidantes; your inner circle will make you or break you. So who belongs in the "council" in this inner circle? Strive for the following:

Creative people
Loyal people
People who share your vision
Wise and intelligent people
People with complementary gifts
People with influence
People of faith
People of integrity

The Maxwell Leadership Bible

Where does God fit in? Leaders and organizations constantly make plans. Yet Isaiah issues a warning to every leader who develops plans without consulting God's design (Isaiah 30:1–5). Leaders must remember just how tentative strategic plans need to be. No one knows the future except God. Keep in mind the following equation as you plan:

Our Preparation + God's Providence = Success

Leaders must constantly ask if their plans fit God's revealed will for them and their organization. Then they must ask if their plans remain relevant to the needs of their mission, their values, their vision, and their long–range objectives. Finally, they need to ask if their plans fit the needs of their culture and time.

The Maxwell Leadership Bible

The Priority of God's Word

The longest chapter in the Bible is a song about the priority of the Word of God. For 176 verses, Psalm 119 holds high the words and wisdom of God and convinces us to treasure it more than anything else in life.

Why is this so crucial for us? Leaders in our world face two realities:

1. Change happens faster than ever, so leaders must remain adaptable.

2. We need timeless values more than ever, so leaders must remain principle driven.

Consider what Psalm 119 teaches about God's Word as our source for leadership principles. Our leadership will . . .

be blessed.

remain pure and ethical.

be strengthened and revitalized.

insightfully answer criticism.

enjoy liberty.

gain wise counsel when needed.

remain steady even when afflicted.

be enlightened, intuitive.

have a reliable guide.

The Maxwell Leadership Bible

This Week: Consider the members of your team. Whose counsel do you trust? Why? Consider your superiors? Do you trust all of them? Why or why not? Do your advisors know how you esteem them? In what areas could you use more or better counselors? Are you a good advisor for others? Remember, "Where there is no counsel, the people fall; but in the multitude of counselors there is safety" (Proverbs 11:14).

GOD'S PROMISE
TO LEADERS

Blessed is the man who trusts in the LORD,
And whose hope is the LORD.
For he shall be like a tree planted by the waters,
Which spreads out its roots by the river,
And will not fear when heat comes;
But its leaf will be green,
And will not be anxious in the year of drought,
Nor will cease from yielding fruit.

JEREMIAH 17:7–8

A LEADER'S PROMISE
TO THE TEAM
I WILL CONTINUALLY GROW
MY LEADERSHIP SKILLS IN ORDER TO BETTER
SERVE OUR TEAM AND OUR CUSTOMERS.

GROWTH STARTS WITH THE LEADER

So when Peter saw it, he responded to the people . . .
Many of those who heard the word believed; and the number
of the men came to be about five thousand.

ACTS 3:12, 4:4

A company cannot grow without, until its leaders grow within. I often am amazed at the money, energy, and marketing that organizations focus on areas that will not produce growth. Slick brochures and catchy slogans will never overcome incompetent leadership.

In 1981 I became senior pastor of a church whose attendance was obviously on a plateau. When I called my first staff meeting, I drew a line across a marker board and wrote the number "1,000." I shared that although I knew the staff could lead one thousand people effectively, I did not know whether they could lead two thousand people. When the leaders changed positively, I knew the growth would become automatic. First, though, I had to help them change themselves.

The strength of any organization is a direct result of the strength of its leaders.

Weak leaders = weak organizations.

Strong leaders = strong organizations.

Everything rises and falls on leadership.

Developing the Leaders Around You

What does it take to have the focus required to be a truly effective leader? The keys are priorities and concentration. To focus your time and energy use these guidelines to help you:

Focus 70 percent on developing strengths. Effective leaders who reach their potential spend more time focusing on what they do well than on what they do wrong.

Focus 25 percent on new things. If you want to get better, you have to keep changing and improving. That means stepping out into new areas. If you dedicate time to new things related to your strength areas, then you'll grow as a leader.

Focus 5 percent on areas of weakness. Nobody can entirely avoid working in areas of weakness. The key is to minimize it as much as possible, and leaders can do it by delegating.

The 21 Indispensable Qualities of a Leader

Encourage others' strengths. If you start trying to help your people grow by correcting their weaknesses, you will demoralize them and unintentionally sabotage the enlarging process. Instead, give your attention to people's strengths. Sharpen skills that already exist. Compliment positive qualities. Bring out the gifts inherent in them. Weaknesses can wait unless they are character flaws. Only after you have developed a strong rapport with the person and they have begun to grow and gain confidence should you address areas of weakness. And then those should be handled gently and one at a time.

Becoming a Person of Influence

GROWTH = CHANGE

Be transformed by the renewing of your mind.

ROMANS 12:2

Change is hard for most people, but growth is impossible without change. Most people fight against change, especially when it affects them personally. As novelist Leo Tolstoy said, "Everyone thinks of changing the world, but no one thinks of changing himself."

Change is inevitable. Everybody has to deal with it in their lives. On the other hand, growth is optional. You can choose to grow or to fight it. But know this: people unwilling to grow will never reach their potential.

Making the change from being an occasional learner to someone dedicated to personal growth is tough. It goes against the grain of the way most people live. Most people celebrate when they receive their diploma or degree and say to themselves, "Thank goodness that's over. I'm done with studying." But that kind of thinking doesn't take you any higher than average.

Your Road Map for Success

THIS WEEK: Reflect on who you are and face your flaws. You can reach your potential tomorrow if you dedicate yourself to growth today. Remember, to change your world, you must first change yourself. To do that:

1. See yourself clearly.
2. Admit your flaws honestly.
3. Discover your strengths joyfully.
4. Build on those strengths passionately.

Failing Forward

GOD'S PROMISE
TO LEADERS

*I will instruct you and teach you
in the way you should go;
I will guide you with My eye.*

PSALM 32:8

A LEADER'S PROMISE
TO THE TEAM

I KNOW WHERE WE NEED TO GO,
AND I CAN GET US THERE.
THIS IS OUR PATH.

IDENTIFY THE VISION

Where there is no vision, the people perish.

PROVERBS 29:18 (KJV)

Have you ever been part of a team that didn't seem to make any progress? Maybe the group had plenty of talent, resources, and opportunities, and team members got along, but the group just never went anywhere. There's a strong possibility that the situation was caused by lack of vision.

Great vision precedes great achievement. Every team needs a compelling vision to give it direction. If a team doesn't have one, then the group is liable to suffer the fate expressed by baseball Hall–of–Famer Yogi Berra: "You've got to be very careful if you don't know where you're going, because you might not get there." A team without vision is, at worst, purposeless. At best, it is subject to the personal—and sometimes selfish—agendas of various teammates. As those agendas work against each other, it saps the team's energy and drive. On the other hand, a team that embraces a vision becomes focused, energized, and confident. It knows where it's headed and why it's going there.

If you lead your team, then you are responsible for identifying a worthy and compelling vision and articulating it to your team members.

The 17 Indisputable Laws of Teamwork

LEADING THE LEADER

Vision is indispensable. It leads the leaders. It paints the targets, sparks and fuels the fire within, and draws them forward. And it is also the fire–lighter for others who follow those leaders. Show me a leader without vision, and I'll show you someone who isn't going anywhere. To get a handle on vision, understand these things:

1. *Vision starts within.* If you lack vision, draw on your calling and your natural gifts and desires. If you still don't sense a vision of your own, then consider partnering with a leader whose vision resonates with you.

2. *Vision draws on your history.* Vision isn't some mystical quality that comes out of a vacuum. It grows out of your past and the history of the people around you.

3. *Vision meets others' needs.* True vision goes beyond what one individual can accomplish. It also does more than just include others; it adds value to them. If your vision doesn't serve others, it's probably too small.

4. *Vision helps you gather resources.* Vision acts like a magnet. It attracts, challenges, and unites people. It also rallies finances and other resources. The greater the vision, the more winners it has the potential to attract. The more challenging the vision, the harder the participants fight to achieve it.

The 21 Indispensable Qualities of a Leader

Know the way, then show the way. Leaders do more than control the direction in which they and their people travel. They see the whole trip in their minds before they set forth. Leaders see *farther* than others see, *more* than others see, and *before* others see.

The Maxwell Leadership Bible

LET THESE VOICES GUIDE YOUR VISION

The Inner Voice. What's your mission? What stirs your heart? If what you're pursuing in life doesn't come from within, you will not be able to accomplish it.

The Unhappy Voice. Discontent with the status quo is a great catalyst for vision. Are you on complacent cruise control? Or do you itch to change your world?

The Successful Voice. Nobody can accomplish great things alone. To fulfill a big vision, you need a good team. But you also need good advice from someone who is ahead of you in the leadership journey. If you want to lead others to greatness, find a good mentor.

The Higher Voice. A truly valuable vision must have God in it. Only He knows what you're really capable of. Have you looked beyond yourself, even beyond your own lifetime as you've sought your vision? If not, you may be missing your true potential and life's best for you.

The 21 Indispensable Qualities of a Leader

THIS WEEK: Draw a "map" of where your team is, where you've been, and where you're going. Note some of the mountains, valleys, deserts, and rivers you've encountered. Does your team know the history of the journey? Are they clear about where you're going and what challenges await?

GOD'S PROMISE
TO LEADERS

I have taught you in the way of wisdom;
I have led you in right paths.
When you walk, your steps will not be hindered,
And when you run, you will not stumble.
Take firm hold of instruction, do not let go;
Keep her, for she is your life.

PROVERBS 4:11–13

A LEADER'S PROMISE
TO THE TEAM

OUR JOURNEY TOGETHER WILL HAVE
DIFFICULT TIMES, BUT I WILL STAY ON A PATH
OF ONGOING GROWTH TO HELP US
MEET THE CHALLENGES AHEAD.

KEEP IMPROVING

Everyone who competes in the games goes into strict training.

1 CORINTHIANS 9:25 (NIV)

We live in a society with destination disease. Too many people want to do enough to "arrive," and then they want to retire. My friend Kevin Myers says it this way: "Everyone is looking for a quick fix, but what they really need is fitness. People who look for fixes stop doing what's right when pressure is relieved. People who pursue fitness do what they should no matter what the circumstances are." People who are constantly improving themselves make three processes an ongoing cycle in their lives.

1. *Preparation.* When individuals are intentional about learning something every day, then they become better prepared to handle whatever challenges they meet.

2. *Contemplation.* Time alone is essential to self–improvement. It allows you to gain perspective on your failures and successes so that you can learn from them. It gives you the time and space to sharpen your personal or organizational vision. And it enables you to plan how you can improve in the future.

3. *Application.* Musician Bruce Springsteen said, "A time comes when you need to stop waiting for the man you want to become and start being the man you want to be." In other words, you need to apply what you've learned.

The 17 Essential Qualities of a Team Player

LEADERS ARE LEARNERS

A wise man will hear and increase learning.

PROVERBS 1:5

If you continually invest in your leadership development, the inevitable result is growth over time. Although it's true that some people are born with greater natural gifts than others, the ability to lead is really a collection of skills, nearly all of which can be learned and improved. But that process doesn't happen overnight. Leadership is complicated. It has many facets: respect, experience, emotional strength, people skills, discipline, vision, momentum, timing—the list goes on. That's why leaders require so much seasoning to be effective.

Successful leaders are learners. And the learning process is ongoing, a result of self–discipline and perseverance. The goal each day must be to get a little better, to build on the previous day's progress.

The 21 Irrefutable Laws of Leadership

When Naaman sought Elisha's help in curing his leprosy, Elisha's response enraged Naaman (2 Kings 5:11). He struggled with pride, faulty expectations, and inflexibility. Yet as a strong leader, Naaman had surrounded himself with individuals who could speak up and disagree with him, and his inner circle provided good counsel. Naaman changed his mind, followed the prophet's directives, and was healed. Leaders who remain teachable receive ongoing blessings.

The Maxwell Leadership Bible

LIFT YOUR LID

When good people run things, everyone is glad,
but when the ruler is bad, everyone groans.

PROVERBS 29:2 (MSG)

Success is within the reach of just about everyone. But personal success without leadership ability brings only limited effectiveness. A person's impact is only a fraction of what it could be with good leadership. The higher you want to climb, the more you need leadership. The greater the impact you want to make, the greater your influence needs to be. Whatever you will accomplish is restricted by your ability to lead others.

Leadership ability is the lid that determines a person's level of effectiveness. The lower a person's ability to lead, the lower the lid on his potential. The higher the leadership, the greater the effectiveness. Your leadership ability—for better or for worse—always determines your effectiveness and the potential impact of your organization. To reach the highest level of effectiveness, you have to raise the lid on your leadership ability. The good news is that you can—if you're willing to pay the price to change.

The 21 Irrefutable Laws of Leadership

THIS WEEK: Evaluate your personal growth journey. Do you have a strategic plan or are you just learning whatever comes your way? List three ways you want to grow, and then list three possible ways to facilitate each growth goal. Are you encouraging your team members to grow strategically?

GOD'S PROMISE
TO LEADERS

So know that the LORD your God is God,
the faithful God. He will keep his agreement of
love for a thousand lifetimes for
people who love him and obey his commands.

DEUTERONOMY 7:9 (NCV)

A LEADER'S PROMISE
TO THE TEAM

I'M COMMITTED TO THE SUCCESSFUL
FULFILLMENT OF OUR STATED MISSION.
WORK WITH ME,
AND WE'LL GET IT DONE RIGHT.

WEEK 30

KEEP YOUR COMMITMENTS

*And it happened, when all our enemies heard of it,
and all the nations around us saw these things, that they were
very disheartened in their own eyes; for they perceived that
this work was done by our God.*

NEHEMIAH 6:16

Commitment comes before anything else in a leader's life. Because Nehemiah had it and drew it out of others, the people finished the wall in fifty–three days, despite much adversity. Their great accomplishment so thrilled Nehemiah that he wrote, "When all our enemies heard of it, and all the nations around us saw these things . . . they were very disheartened in their own eyes; for they perceived that this work was done by our God."

Leaders who complete a task possess these characteristics:

Compelling purpose. They make a great commitment to a great cause.

Clear perspective. They don't let fear cloud their view of the future.

Continual prayer. They pray about everything and gain God's favor.

Courageous persistence. They move ahead despite the odds.

If you're facing a God–sized challenge, cultivate these characteristics to give yourself the best opportunity for success.

The Maxwell Leadership Bible

Commitment Precedes Resources

But Ruth said: "Entreat me not to leave you,
Or to turn back from following after you;
For wherever you go, I will go; And wherever you lodge,
I will lodge; Your people shall be my people,
And your God, my God."

RUTH 1:16

While every leader needs financial and human resources
to reach his or her goals, commitment should always precede
those resources. When a leader demonstrates a commitment
to the mission and goals of the organization, then God
moves and a whole stream of events begin to flow.

In the very first chapter of the book that bears her name,
Ruth chooses to stay with Naomi, her mother–in–law, even
after she loses her husband. She didn't know it, but her
commitment would lead to all kinds of open doors. Ruth
finds work during a difficult time, makes friends in a foreign
land, and eventually gains a new husband, Boaz. Most
impressively, God includes her—a Moabite adopted into
the family of Israel—in the line of Christ. The child she
bore became part of the lineage of the Messiah.

The key? Commitment. Once a leader definitely
commits, God moves and all manner of unforeseen
incidents, meetings, persons, and material assistance begin
to stream forth.

The Maxwell Leadership Bible

I know whom I have believed, and am persuaded that He is able to keep that which I have committed unto Him, against that day.

GO THE DISTANCE

Genesis 11:31 tells us that Abraham's father, Terah, set out for Canaan from Ur of the Chaldeans long before Abraham made a similar trip. But for some reason, Terah stopped in Haran and never continued his journey. Did Terah receive an original call from God . . . but neglect to follow through? We don't know.

We do know that Abraham never made such a mistake. Although he made other leadership errors, Abraham always seemed to follow through on his commitments. When God called him to depart to an unknown land, he went the distance. When enemies abducted Lot and his goods, Abraham pursued the kidnappers and subdued them (Genesis 14:14–16). When commanded to circumcise the males of his household, Abraham did it that very day (Genesis 17:23). And when God asked Abraham to sacrifice his beloved son, Isaac, only a last–second angelic intervention spared the young man's life (Genesis 22:1–9). No wonder that God, the Ultimate Leader, called Abraham "My friend" (Isaiah 41:8)!

The Maxwell Leadership Bible

THIS WEEK: List some of your commitments at work, at home, and in the community. Are you going the distance in all of them? Which commitments do you wish you could drop or change? Is your team confident in your commitment to them and to your mission? What are the boundaries of your commitments?

Father, Education is not my Savior, your beloved Son is my Savior.

Obeying Him must be my commitment

GOD'S PROMISE
TO LEADERS

*Let heaven fill your thoughts. Do not think only
about things down here on earth. For you
died when Christ died, and your real life
is hidden with Christ in God. And when Christ,
who is your real life, is revealed to the
whole world, you will share in all his glory.*

COLOSSIANS 3:2–4 (NLT)

A LEADER'S PROMISE
TO THE TEAM

I WILL ASK QUESTIONS, SEEK ANSWERS,
AND KNOCK ON ALL DOORS UNTIL
I'M CONFIDENT THAT WE'RE
PURSUING THE RIGHT PURPOSE.

KNOW YOUR PURPOSE

*For we are His workmanship, created in Christ Jesus
for good works, which God prepared beforehand
that we should walk in them.*

EPHESIANS 2:10

Nothing in life can take the place of knowing your purpose. If you don't try to discover your purpose, you're likely to spend your life doing the wrong things.

I believe that God created every person for a purpose. As psychologist Viktor Frankl said, "Everyone has his own specific vocation or mission in life. . . . Thus everyone's task is as unique as his specific opportunity to implement it." Each of us has a purpose for which we were created. Our responsibility—and our joy—is to identify it.

Here are some questions to ask yourself to help you identify your purpose:

For what am I searching? All of us have a strong desire set in our hearts, something that speaks to our deepest thoughts and feelings, something that sets our souls on fire.

Why was I created? Think about the unique mix of abilities you have, the resources available to you, your own personal history, and the opportunities around you.

Do I believe in my potential? No one can consistently act in a manner inconsistent with the way he sees himself.

When do I start? The answer to that question is "NOW."

Your Road Map for Success

THE POWER OF PURPOSE

The apostle Paul might have been forgiven had he chosen to take a little sabbatical as he sat in prison, awaiting his trial. Yet he used even this opportunity to advance the gospel (Philippians 1:12–14). Paul was a leader who never drifted from his mission. He determined to leave his mark wherever he went.

How did Paul's sense of purpose keep him in the battle as he sat in prison? What did he learn behind bars? Consider the following:

A purpose will motivate you.
A purpose will keep your priorities straight.
A purpose will develop your potential.
A purpose will give you power to live in the present.
A purpose will help you evaluate your progress.

The Maxwell Leadership Bible

Seek God, then ask these questions. Most people can prioritize when faced with right or wrong issues. The challenge arises when we are faced with two good choices. If you're having trouble deciding between two good things, then look at these suggestions.

Ask your overseer or coworkers their preference.

Can one of the options be handled by someone else?

Which option would be of greater benefit to the customer?

Make your decision based on the purpose of the organization.

Developing the Leader Within You

TRADING FOR SOMETHING GREATER

Poet Rudyard Kipling said, "If you don't get what you want, it is a sign either that you did not seriously want it, or that you tried to bargain over the price." How badly do you want to reach your potential and fulfill your purpose in life? It will take passion on your part to keep growing, learning, and trading up.

Over the years I've found that you have to make tradeoffs throughout life in order to succeed, and only through wise exchanges can you reach your potential.

The problem of many unsuccessful people is that they haven't worked to develop much in their lives worth trading. You can only make a trade when you've got something worth giving up. And when you do trade, you don't trade from the lowest level to the highest, skipping over all the levels in between. Usually you're only able to move one level at a time—either up or down.

Your Road Map for Success

THIS WEEK: Meditate on Revelation 12:12–13: "And behold, I am coming quickly, and My reward is with Me, to give to every one according to his work. I am the Alpha and the Omega, the Beginning and the End, the First and the Last." What does this say about how God wants us to prioritize Him? Is He in every part of your life? In other words, does your priority list read like this: God and family, God and job, God and church, God and community, and so forth?

GOD'S PROMISE
TO LEADERS

*There is going to come a time of testing at the
judgment day to see what kind of work
each builder has done. Everyone's work will be
put through the fire to see whether or not it keeps
its value. If the work survives the fire,
that builder will receive a reward. But if the
work is burned up, the builder will suffer great loss.
The builders themselves will be saved, but like
someone escaping through a wall of flames.*

1 CORINTHIANS 3:13–15 (NLT)

A LEADER'S PROMISE
TO THE TEAM

I WILL VALUE YOU AS PEOPLE,
PRAISE YOUR EFFORTS, AND REWARD YOU
BASED ON YOUR PERFORMANCE.

LEAD FROM THE INSIDE OUT

*So he shepherded them according to the integrity of his heart,
and guided them by the skillfulness of his hands.*

PSALM 78:72

D avid's leadership succeeded through a two–sided coin:
his outward skill and his inward integrity. Every great
leader must have this combination. Leaders must . . .

1. Value excellence.
2. Not settle for average.
3. Pay attention to detail.
4. Remain committed to what really matters.
5. Display integrity and sound ethics.
6. Show genuine respect for others.
7. Go the second mile.
8. Demonstrate consistency.
9. Never stop improving
10. Always give 100%.
11. Make excellence a lifestyle.

The first person you lead is you—and you can't lead
effectively without self–discipline. Leaders must . . .

1. Develop and follow your priorities.
2. Challenge your excuses.
3. Remove rewards until you finish the job.
4. Stay focused on results, and never trade what you
want at the moment for what you want most.

The Maxwell Leadership Bible

COMPETENCE DOESN'T COMPENSATE
FOR INSECURITY

So from that time on Saul kept a jealous eye on David.

1 SAMUEL 18:9 (NLT)

Insecure leaders are dangerous—to themselves, their followers, and the organizations they lead. That's because a leadership position becomes an amplifier of personal flaws. Whatever negative baggage you have in life only gets heavier when you're trying to lead others.

Unsure leaders have several common traits:

1. *They don't provide security for others.* To become an effective leader, you need to make your followers feel good about themselves.

2. *They take more from people than they give.* Insecure people are on a continual quest for validation, acknowledgment, and love. Because of that, their focus is on finding security, not instilling it in others.

3. *They continually limit their best people.* Show me an insecure leader, and I'll show you someone who cannot genuinely celebrate victories. The leader might even take credit personally for the best work of the team.

4. *They continually limit their organization.* When followers are undermined and receive no recognition, they become discouraged and eventually stop performing at their potential. And when that happens, the entire organization suffers.

The 21 Indispensable Qualities of a Leader

LOVE PEOPLE, REWARD PERFORMANCE

*"Well done, good and faithful servant; you have been
faithful over a few things, I will make you
ruler over many things. Enter into the joy of your lord."*

MATTHEW 25:23

Educators in the United States have been seeking ways to increase students' test scores. One popular theory states that the best way to improve children's ability is to puff up their self–esteem because high achievers tend to have high self–esteem. However, researchers have found that simply building children's egos breeds many negative traits: indifference to excellence, inability to overcome adversity, and aggressiveness toward people who criticize them.

Now, I place high value on praising people, especially children. But I also believe that you have to base your praise on truth. Here's the approach I use to encourage and lead others:

Value people. Praise effort. Reward performance.

I use that method with everyone, including myself.

Failing Forward

THIS WEEK: Do you have clearly defined standards of excellence for you and your team? Does everyone understand what those standards are? How well are you meeting those standards? In what ways are you struggling? What can you as a leader do to improve performance? What does your team think?

GOD'S PROMISE
TO LEADERS

Have I not commanded you?
Be strong and of good courage;
do not be afraid, nor be dismayed, for the LORD
your God is with you wherever you go.

JOSHUA 1:9

A LEADER'S PROMISE
TO THE TEAM

I KNOW THE DANGERS ALONG OUR PATH,
AND I KNOW WE CAN OVERCOME THEM.

LEAD WITH COURAGE

"Be strong and of good courage . . ."

DEUTERONOMY 31:7

Whenever you see significant progress in an organization, it's because the leader made courageous decisions. The leadership position itself doesn't give people courage, but courage can give them a leadership position. As you approach the tough decisions that will challenge you, recognize these truths about courage:

1. Courage begins with an inward battle. Courage isn't an absence of fear; it's doing what you are afraid to do.

2. Courage is making things right, not just smoothing them over. Martin Luther King, Jr. said, "The ultimate measure of a man is not where he stands in moments of comfort and convenience, but where he stands at times of challenge and controversy."

3. Courage in a leader inspires commitment from followers. "Courage is contagious," says evangelist Billy Graham. "When a brave man takes a stand, the spines of others are stiffened."

4. Your life expands in proportion to your courage. Roman historian Tacitus said, "The desire for safety stands against every great and noble enterprise." But courage opens doors, and that's one of its most wonderful benefits.

The 21 Indispensable Qualities of a Leader

WHERE IS YOUR CONFIDENCE?

It's always a good idea to have a battle plan if you intend to lead an army into war. Moses possessed a plan for the army of Israel, a set of instructions that came straight from the very top (Deuteronomy 20:1). Imagine the confidence a field commander could instill in his troops knowing that he could not lose. That was just the kind of guarantee God gave Moses and the people of Israel. God assured them they had nothing to fear—as long as they remembered that He would remain with them always.

Christian leaders today can bank on the same promise that gave Moses such courage: "For the Lord your God is He who goes with you, to fight for you against your enemies, to save you" (Deuteronomy 20:4). And so God gives us the same words He gave to Moses: "Do not be afraid."

Take the necessary risks. True leadership may mean standing alone and speaking difficult truth. The prophet Elijah knew this well as he prayed for judgment on his own people, confronted a wicked king, then challenged hundreds of false prophets. He risked his life to lead Israel back to God (1 Kings 18:37). Risks are tough for most people. This is why leaders must both model courage and call it forth from others.

The Maxwell Leadership Bible

FALLING SHORT

Then Saul said to Samuel, "I have sinned, for I have
transgressed the commandment of the LORD and your words,
because I feared the people and obeyed their voice."

1 SAMUEL 15:24

King Saul never won the inward battles. When faced
with a challenge he panicked. He lacked the courage
necessary to lead the people of Israel.

Some lessons about courage we learn from Saul are that:

Courage and cowardice are both contagious. When
Saul fled, so did his men.

Without courage, it doesn't matter how good your
intentions are. Saul had good intentions when he presented
burnt offerings to the Lord. But he let his fear that people
would desert him control his actions.

Without courage, we're slaves of our own insecurity
and possessiveness. Saul was captive to his fears of being
replaced by David.

A leader without courage will never let go of the familiar.
Saul employed a medium to ask counsel of Samuel's spirit.

Lack of courage will eventually sabotage a leader. Saul's
lack of courage cost him everything.

The Maxwell Leadership Bible

THIS WEEK: Consider the risks before you. What does
your team fear? What do you fear? How can you increase
your courage and model it more for your team?

GOD'S PROMISE
TO LEADERS

Now He who searches the hearts knows
what the mind of the Spirit is, because He makes
intercession for the saints according to the will
of God. And we know that all things work
together for good to those who love God, to those
who are the called according to His purpose.

ROMANS 8:27–28

A LEADER'S PROMISE
TO THE TEAM

I GENUINELY CARE ABOUT EVERYONE
ON THIS TEAM AND ABOUT
WHAT WE'RE ACCOMPLISHING TOGETHER.

LEADERSHIP BEGINS
IN THE HEART

No longer do I call you servants . . .
but I have called you friends.

JOHN 15:15

What can a person do to manage and cultivate good relationships as a leader? It requires three things:

1. *Understand people.* Marketing expert Rod Nichols says, "If you deal with every customer in the same way, you will only close 25 percent to 30 percent of your contacts, because you will only close one personality type. But if you learn how to effectively work with all four personality types, you can conceivably close 100 percent of your contacts."

2. *Love people.* Businessman Henry Gruland says, "Being a leader is more than just wanting to lead. Leaders have empathy for others and a keen ability to find the best in people . . . not the worst . . . by truly caring for others." You cannot be a truly effective leader unless you love people.

3. *Help people.* If your focus is on what you can put into people rather than what you can get out of them, they'll love and respect you—and those attributes are great foundations for building relationships.

The 21 Indispensable Qualities of a Leader

A Leader's Heart

The selection of David to be Israel's king illustrates how God often disregards human customs and traditions to accomplish His purposes (1 Samuel 16:7). God saw the heart of this young man and knew that His people needed a leader with a tenderness of spirit. David might have become a warrior, but gentleness was his defining trait. David's life illustrates that faithfulness in small things often results in much larger assignments and greater responsibility down the road. David loved the Lord and lived his life as a man after God's own heart.

Who you are precedes what you do. As Paul spoke to the Ephesians in Acts 20:22–24, he described the ingredients of an effective leader. Paul made tough calls, yet shed tears in front of his people. One thing is sure: Leadership begins with the heart. Paul had a heart that was . . .

Consistent. He lived steadily while moving among the people he led.

Contrite. He acted humbly and willingly showed his weakness.

Courageous. He didn't shrink from doing the right thing.

Convictional. He communicated his convictions boldly.

Committed. He left for Jerusalem, willing to die for Jesus.

Captivated. He showed that a surrendered man doesn't have to survive.

The Maxwell Leadership Bible

WHOLE–HEARTED DEVOTION

Whatever you do, work at it with all your heart,
as working for the Lord, not for men.

COLOSSIANS 3:23 (NIV)

Experts spend a lot of time trying to figure out what makes people successful, and more than anything else, passion is what makes the difference.

Take a look at four truths about passion and what it can do for you as a leader:

1. *Passion is the first step to achievement.* Your desire determines your destiny. The stronger your fire, the greater the desire—and the greater the potential.

2. *Passion increases your willpower.* There is no substitute for passion. It is fuel for the will. If you want anything badly enough, you can find the willpower to achieve it.

3. *Passion changes you.* If you follow your passion you can't help but become a more dedicated, productive person. In the end, your passion will have more influence than your personality.

4. *Passion makes the impossible possible.* Human beings are so made that whenever anything fires their soul, impossibilities vanish. A fire in the heart lifts everything in your life A leader with great passion and few skills always outperforms a leader with great skills and no passion.

The 21 Indispensable Qualities of a Leader

THIS WEEK: Give your heart a checkup. About what are you passionate? Is your heart consistent, contrite, courageous, convictional, committed, and captivated?

GOD'S PROMISE TO LEADERS

*Therefore, L*ORD *God of Israel, now keep what You promised Your servant David my father, saying, "You shall not fail to have a man sit before Me on the throne of Israel, only if your sons take heed to their way, that they walk in My law as you have walked before Me."*

2 CHRONICLES 6:16

A LEADER'S PROMISE TO THE TEAM

I WILL HELP PREPARE OTHER LEADERS
TO RISE TO NEW LEVELS
OF RESPONSIBILITY AND INFLUENCE.

LEAVE A LEADERSHIP LEGACY

And the LORD said to Moses: "Take Joshua the son of Nun with you, a man in whom is the Spirit, and lay your hand on him; set him before Eleazar the priest and before all the congregation, and inaugurate him in their sight. And you shall give some of your authority to him, that all the congregation of the children of Israel may be obedient.

NUMBERS 27:18–20

Of all the wonderful ways Moses expressed his leadership, the most strategic had to be his training of Joshua. Moses passed along his authority, abilities, and anointing to Joshua. He gave Joshua his time, his insight, a learning environment, an opportunity to prove himself, and a strong belief in his future.

The interaction of Moses and Joshua demonstrates that reproducing leaders is not a quick, simple process. It requires time, emotional investment, and sacrifice.

When you begin developing the next generation of leaders, recognize that your protégés will need certain things:

1. From themselves: Conviction, courage, and obedience
2. From their mentor: Equipping
3. From God: Vision
4. From the people: Buy–In

With time, investment, and sacrifice, you will build a legacy of leadership.

The Maxwell Leadership Bible

Leave More than an Inheritance

A huge difference exists between a legacy and an inheritance. Anyone can leave an inheritance. An inheritance is something you leave to your family or loved ones. (It also fades.) A legacy is something you leave in your family and loved ones. Consider these differences:

INHERITANCE	LEGACY
1. Something you give to others	1. Something you place in others
2. Temporarily brings them happiness	2. Permanently transforms them
3. Eventually fades as it is spent	3. Lives on long after you die
4. Your activity may or may not pay off	4. Your activity becomes achievement

The Maxwell Leadership Bible

You reap what you sow. In trying to encourage the Corinthian church to give generously, the apostle Paul instructs the church to view its resources as a farmer views his sowing seed (2 Corinthians 9:10–11). You can't harvest what you haven't planted. Some leaders, like the Corinthians, find it hard to invest resources because they fear their commodities will run out. Good leaders see the same resources as sufficient seed to be sown—knowing the harvest will come and more will be created. We must guard against poverty; we should give our life because it is plentiful.

The Maxwell Leadership Bible

A HOUSE DIVIDED

Saul's death led to all kinds of turmoil over who would become the next king. Despite David's anointing by Samuel, others saw a tempting opportunity to seize power (2 Samuel 2:10).

Transitions often bring difficult times. Leaders who fail to plan for their departure invite trouble. Saul could have been a hero had he cooperated with God in preparing David to succeed him. He didn't have a more submissive staff person in his entire palace than David. Saul could've helped himself had he recognized these truths:

1. Leaders must see ahead and prepare for change.
2. People can live without certainty, but not without clarity regarding future direction.
3. Wise choices today put "change in the pocket" of a leader regarding future choices.
4. Problem–solving skills and effective communication earn the leader trust and credibility.

The Maxwell Leadership Bible

THIS WEEK: Consider your leadership heritage. What legacies are you fulfilling? Read the first nine chapters of 1 Chronicles to see a genealogy of Israel's leaders. How can you apply the following lessons from that lineage to your life?

They remained connected to their heritage.

They gained perspective from their place in history.

They were able to honor their forefathers.

They saw their lineage as a family blessing.

They sensed tendencies of ancestral giftedness and calling.

They could retain their identity even when exiled.

The Maxwell Leadership Bible

GOD'S PROMISE
TO LEADERS

Blessed is the man who listens to me,
Watching daily at my gates,
Waiting at the posts of my doors.
For whoever finds me finds life,
And obtains favor from the LORD.

PROVERBS 8:34–35

A LEADER'S PROMISE
TO THE TEAM

YOU ARE IMPORTANT TO ME, TO THIS TEAM,
AND TO OUR MISSION. I WANT TO HEAR WHAT
YOU HAVE TO SAY. I WILL LISTEN.

LISTEN UP

*. . . and after the earthquake a fire, but the LORD
was not in the fire; and after the fire a still small voice.
So it was, when Elijah heard it."*

1 KINGS 19:12–13

S omeone once asked Joan of Arc why God spoke only to her. She responded, "Sir, you are wrong. God speaks to everyone. I just listen."

When God spoke to Samuel, it was as the boy lay down quietly in the middle of the night. Even then, Samuel did not at first recognize that the voice belonged to God. He needed the wisdom of his experienced mentor, Eli, to understand who was communicating with him. But based on how often Samuel heard God's voice as an adult, it's clear that he did learn to identify, listen to, and obey God's voice.

Leaders are often very busy people. And they can easily get caught up in the activity of their obligations. If you're a leader, that's why it's important to set aside times to quiet yourself and listen for God's direction.

The 21 Most Powerful Minutes in a Leader's Day

WHEN A LEADER SPEAKS

When somebody asks a question in a meeting, whom do people look to for the answer? This person is the real leader.

Identifying a real leader can be easy if you remember what you're looking for. Don't listen to the claims of the person professing to be the leader. Instead, observe the reactions of the people around him. The proof of leadership is found in the followers. People listen to what someone has to say not necessarily because of the message, but because of their respect for the messenger.

So I must ask you this: How do people react when you communicate? When you speak, do people really listen? Or do they wait to hear what someone else has to say before they act? You can find out a lot about your level of leadership if you have the courage to ask and answer that question.

The 21 Irrefutable Laws of Leadership

To communicate, listen. For one whole week, Job's friends just sat with him and listened (Job 2:11–13). They realized an important truth: People don't lose intimacy when they stop talking, but when they stop listening. Leaders seldom realize how much their listening empowers the other person. Because they are leaders, the sheer act of listening speaks volumes that even a great speech can't communicate.

The Maxwell Leadership Bible

SPEAK UP TO YOUR LEADER

Good leaders cultivate honest speech;
they love advisors who tell them the truth.

PROVERBS 16:13 (MSG)

Good team leaders never want yes–men. They need direct and honest communication from their people. I have always encouraged people on my team to speak openly and directly with me. Our meetings are often brainstorming sessions where the best idea wins. Often, a team member's remarks or observations really help the team. Sometimes we disagree. That's okay, because we've developed strong enough relationships that we can survive conflict. Getting everything out on the table always improves the team. The one thing I never want to hear from a teammate is, "I could have told you that wouldn't work." If you know it beforehand, that's the time to say it.

Besides directness, the other quality team members need to display when communicating with their leaders is respect. Leading a team isn't easy. It requires making tough and sometimes unpopular decisions. We should respect the people who take on leadership roles and show them loyalty.

The 17 Indisputable Laws of Teamwork

THIS WEEK: Take the time to listen—really listen—to several of your key team members. If they're not coming to you, ask them questions about something. Then ask yourself why they weren't coming to you in the first place. Are you a good listener? Do people really listen to you in meetings or do they listen more to someone else?

GOD'S PROMISE TO LEADERS

But those who wait on the LORD
Shall renew their strength;
They shall mount up with wings like eagles,
They shall run and not be weary,
They shall walk and not faint.

ISAIAH 40:31

A LEADER'S PROMISE
TO THE TEAM

I WILL MANAGE MY TIME
TO THE BEST OF MY ABILITY.
I WILL ENDEAVOR TO MAKE DECISIONS
TO BEST BENEFIT THE TEAM.

MAKE THE MOST
OF YOUR TIME

Lord, make me to know my end, and what is the measure
of my days, that I may know how frail I am. Indeed, You have
made my days as handbreadths, and my age is as nothing
before You; certainly every man at his best state is but vapor.

PSALM 39:4–5

In Psalm 90, David shows his mindfulness of his brief time on earth. He asks God to help him number his days, which ought to be the prayer of every leader. Wise leaders work to redeem the time they have.

A leader needs to wonder if the task is worth the time investment. What would happen if the leader wasn't the one doing it? Is there someone else who could do it just as well, and for whom the task would be time better spent? A good leader knows that time is like gold, and good "spending habits" are essential. It's just that in this case the units are minutes, not dollars.

If you don't know where your time goes—that's a danger signal. If you can save small bits of time and consolidate them into a chunk of time that can be spent on something worthwhile—that's like "found money." If leaders can number their minutes and hours, "numbering their days" will be easier.

The Maxwell Leadership Bible

Do the Right Thing at the Right Time

Good leaders understand that timing is everything. Nehemiah began praying about the ruined wall in December, but not until April did he approach the king about rebuilding them. What was he waiting on?

No one knows for sure, but Nehemiah might well have been waiting on . . .

1. His ownership of the vision and burden.
2. A foundation of prayer to be laid.
3. His own readiness with a plan.
4. The king's mental and emotional mood.
5. The season when he could move quickly.
6. A trust to deepen between him and the king.

Moses felt weary of the complaining, the stagnation, and the lack of progress among his people. He was running on empty. And in his weakened condition he made a decision that cost him his future in the Promised Land (Numbers 20:12). This sad incident teaches us at least two lessons. First, never make a major decision during an emotionally low time. Second, choose to be proactive, not reactive, in your leadership. Get your cues from God and the mission He has given you. Ask yourself these questions:

1. Am I a reactor or a creator when I lead?
2. Do I play defense or offense when I lead?
3. Am I a people–pleaser or a God–pleaser when I lead?
4. Do I boss my calendar, or does someone else choose where I give my time?

The Maxwell Leadership Bible

GUARD AGAINST THE SLUGGARD

The lazy man will not plow because of winter;
He will beg during harvest and have nothing.

PROVERBS 20:4

King Solomon had plenty to say about the "sluggard," or the habitually lazy person. The sluggard's only commitment is to his leisure. He avoids honest labor. He contributes nothing to the world; instead, he just pillages some of its resources. When leaders become lazy and lose their diligence in doing good for God, they become spiritual sluggards and worthless to the kingdom.

Wise leaders know their time is limited. They know they have no way to retrieve misused or wasted time (John 9:4). Leaders in the body of Christ must remain diligent in doing good and in encouraging others to do likewise.

The Maxwell Leadership Bible

THIS WEEK: How do you know when to move in leadership? How does asking at the right time increase your chance for success? Read Ecclesiastes chapter 3, which begins with the famous line, "To everything there is a season . . . a time to be born, and a time to die." Consider also how that passage ends: "God shall judge the righteous and the wicked, for there is a time for every purpose and for every work" (v. 17). Is your use of time righteous or wicked?

GOD'S PROMISE
TO LEADERS

Trust in the LORD, and do good;
Dwell in the land, and feed on His faithfulness.
Delight yourself also in the LORD,
And He shall give you the desires of your heart.

PSALM 37:3–4

A LEADER'S PROMISE
TO THE TEAM

I WILL GUARD MY CHARACTER,
TAKE RESPONSIBILITY FOR DECISIONS,
AND CONSISTENTLY TRY TO DO THE RIGHT
THING. I WON'T PRETEND TO BE PERFECT,
BUT I WILL DEMONSTRATE THAT I AM
RELIABLE AND WORTHY OF YOUR TRUST.

PASS THE TRUST TEST

Among leaders who lack insight, abuse abounds,
but for one who hates corruption, the future is bright.

PROVERBS 28:16 (MSG)

People today are desperate for leaders, but they want to be influenced by someone they can trust, a person of good character. If you want to become someone who can positively influence other people:

Model consistency of character. Solid trust can only develop when people can trust you all the time

Employ honest communication. To be trustworthy, you have to be like a good musical composition: your words and music must match.

Value transparency. If you're honest with people and admit your weaknesses, they appreciate your honesty. And they are able to relate to you better.

Exemplify humility. People won't trust you if they see that you are driven by ego, jealousy, or the belief that you are better than they are.

Demonstrate your support of others. Nothing develops or displays your character better than your desire to put others first.

Fulfill your promises. One of the fastest ways to break trust with others is in failing to fulfill your commitments.

Becoming a Person of Influence

ACCEPT THE RESPONSIBILITY
OF A LEADER'S TRUST

A leader can delegate anything except responsibility. Leaders simply cannot give it away. They can model it; they can teach it; they can share it. But in the words of Harry Truman, the buck stops with the leader. Then especially in times of crisis, we find out the quality of our leadership.

1. *Dropouts* give up and fail to take responsibility.
2. *Cop–outs* make excuses for why they aren't responsible.
3. *Hold–outs* waiver too long to take responsibility.
4. *All–outs* own the responsibility and take action.

Be a good follower first. Before David became king, he showed respect for his predecessor (1 Samuel 26:9). Saul failed to practice this principle, and lost his kingdom. The Bible provides a vivid contrast between the leadership of Saul and David.

SAUL	DAVID
Was self–conscious from the beginning	Displayed God–confidence from the beginning
Presumed the priestly office	Didn't assume any right or privilege
Disobeyed God in the little things	Obeyed God in the little things
Lost integrity by covering his sin	Maintained integrity by respecting Saul
Failed to submit to God–given authority	Consistently submitted to authority
Was preoccupied with his own fame	Desired to increase God's reputation

The Maxwell Leadership Bible

TRUST BUSTER

Samson learned the hard way that trust provides the foundation for all genuine leadership. This impetuous, volatile, lustful, moody, emotional, and unpredictable man provides a very good example of a very bad leader. Because no one could trust him, none followed his leadership (Judges 15:11–12).

Leaders who erode the solid ground of trustworthy leadership usually exhibit one or more of the following signs—Samson displayed them all. Leaders in trouble . . .

1. fail to address glaring character weaknesses.
2. count on deception to safeguard themselves.
3. act impulsively.
4. are overcome by an area of weakness.
5. misuse their God–given gifts.

Samson's self–centered, undisciplined, and arrogant nature made him an ineffective leader.

The Maxwell Leadership Bible

THIS WEEK: Consider the trustworthiness of the Ultimate Leader. God expects us to obey Him. Why? Because His Word not only keeps us clean—or holy—before Him, but it also protects us and qualifies us for greater blessings. The Father always knows what is best for us and for our relationship with Him. *"If you walk in My statutes and keep My commandments, and perform them, then I will give you rain in its season, the land shall yield its produce, and the trees of the field shall yield their fruit . . . I will walk among you and be your God, and you shall be My people"* (Leviticus 26:3, 4, 12).

GOD'S PROMISE
TO LEADERS

I, the LORD, search the heart,
I test the mind,
Even to give every man according to his ways,
According to the fruit of his doings.

JEREMIAH 17:10

A LEADER'S PROMISE
TO THE TEAM

I RECOGNIZE THAT THE SMALL MATTERS OF
MY HEART CAN MAKE A BIG DIFFERENCE IN OUR
SUCCESS OR FAILURE, SO I'M GUARDING MY
HEART TO KEEP IT IN LINE WITH HIGH VALUES.

PEOPLE WILL FOLLOW THE LEADER

He did evil in the sight of the LORD,
and walked in the way of Jeroboam, and in his sin
by which he had made Israel sin.

1 KINGS 15:34

L eadership ability is the lid on the success of a nation or organization. When Israel or Judah lived under good kings, things went well. Under bad kings, things went sour. The heart and skill of a leader will always tremendously affect the life of the people under his direction. This is a law, both timeless and universal. See how this law played out under the Hebrew kings of the Old Testament:

GOOD KINGS	BAD KINGS
1. Drew loyalty from their people	1. Drew rebellion from their people
2. Enjoyed victory over sin	2. Saw bondage to sin
3. Enjoyed peace within the kingdom	3. Suffered turmoil within the kingdom
4. Were affirmed by God's prophets	4. Were rebuked by God's prophets
5. Enjoyed prosperity	5. Often endured natural disasters and war
6. Opposed evil kings	6. Opposed good kings

The Maxwell Leadership Bible

Why was David able to stand against Goliath when the army of Israel pulled back in fear? Because in the following ways, he differed from others:

1. *Perspective.* He saw an opportunity.

2. *Methods.* He decided to use proven weapons that he knew would work.

3. *Conviction.* He heard Goliath's threats against the God of Israel and knew God could beat him.

4. *Vision.* He wanted to make Yahweh known to the world as the most powerful God on earth.

5. *Experience.* He brought to the battlefield past victories over a lion and bear, not months of paralyzing fear.

6. *Attitude.* He saw Goliath not as a threat too big to hit, but a target too big to miss.

Deception, more often than mistakes, disqualifies leaders. David wrote Psalm 51 shortly after he committed adultery with Bathsheba and had Uriah killed (2 Samuel 11). When Nathan confronted him about his sin (2 Samuel 12), the king publicly sought restoration, so God allowed him to remain in office until he died. Leaders who do not repent after some failure—or who do so only for public show—often lose their positions. History teaches that people usually forgive a leader who owns up to his mistakes, but they refuse to forgive those who remain unrepentant.

The Maxwell Leadership Bible

Leadership in God's Economy

Some leaders step into positions of power out of love and a sense of mission. Others seek leadership merely to gain power over others and feel superior. Normally it doesn't take long to determine which sort of leader you've got. Leaders are not given authority in order to better themselves, enlarge their income or social status, or improve their standard of living. They are first and always servants of others. This idea appears throughout the Scripture.

Human Economy	God's Economy
1. Pursuit of power and prestige.	1. Pursuit of love and service to others.
2. Improve wealth and status of the leader.	2. Improve the welfare of the people.
3. See others as enemies and competitors.	3. See others as brothers who complement.
4. Motive is to remove or kill opposition.	4. Motive is to meet needs and grow the cause.
5. The result: the leader is glorified.	5. The result: God is glorified.

The Maxwell Leadership Bible

THIS WEEK: Reflect on your team. By looking at them, would you say you're a good king? How are you helping your team to be an army of Davids? Are you burdened by some deception? What's your "economic status" according to God?

GOD'S PROMISE
FOR LEADERS

*God is fair; he will not forget the work you did
and the love you showed for him by helping
his people. And he will remember that you are
still helping them. We want each of you to go on
with the same hard work all your lives so you will
surely get what you hope for. We do not want you
to become lazy. Be like those who through faith
and patience will receive what God has promised.*

HEBREWS 6:10–12 (NCV)

A LEADER'S PROMISE
FOR THE TEAM

I WON'T JUST FOLLOW UP ON OUR MISSION;
I'LL FOLLOW THROUGH WITH IT
ALL THE WAY TO THE END,
AND I WILL HELP YOU DO THAT, TOO.

PERSISTENCE PAYS OFF

And it happened, when our enemies heard that it was known
to us, and that God had brought their plot to nothing,
that all of us returned to the wall, everyone to his work.

NEHEMIAH 4:15

One of the great tests of leadership is how you handle opposition. Nehemiah faced the usual tactics of the opposition: ridicule, resistance, and rumor. Nehemiah modeled the right response to all three of these challenges by . . .

Relying on God.

Respecting the opposition.

Reinforcing his weak points.

Reassuring the people.

Refusing to quit.

Renewing the people's strength continually.

Nehemiah had to deal with problems from without—ridicule, resistance, and rumor—and within—disputes about food, property, and taxes.

Persistence is the ultimate gauge of our leadership; the secret is to outlast our critics. Nehemiah taught us this lesson by staying committed to his ultimate calling.

The Maxwell Leadership Bible

THE WILL TO DO WHAT'S RIGHT

Discipline is doing what you really don't want to do, so that you can do what you really want to do. It's paying the price in the little things so that you can buy the bigger thing. Disciplined leaders must possess . . .

1. *Disciplined Thinking.* Keep your mind active and regularly take on mental challenges to develop the kind of disciplined thinking that will help you with whatever you endeavor to do.

2. *Disciplined Emotions.* You must master your emotions or they'll master you. Don't let your feelings prevent you from doing what you should or drive you to do things you shouldn't.

3. *Disciplined Actions.* Action separates the winners from the losers. Your actions always reflect your degree of discipline.

The 17 Essential Qualities of a Team Player

Pay now, play later. When it comes to self–discipline, people choose one of two things—either they choose the pain of discipline, which comes from sacrifice and growth, or they choose the pain of regret, which comes from taking the easy road and missing opportunities. Each person in life chooses. Every person on the planet is given the same allotment of minutes in a day. But each person's level of self–discipline dictates how effectively those minutes are used. Disciplined people maximize the use of their time.

Developing the Leaders Around You

THE LONGEST WAY IS A SHORT–CUT

One of the most common obstacles to success is the desire to cut corners. But shortcuts never pay off in the long run.

If you find that you continually give in to your moods or impulses, then you need to change your approach to doing things. Cutting corners is really a sign of impatience and poor self–discipline. But if you are willing to follow through, you can achieve a breakthrough. The best method is to set up standards for yourself that require accountability. Any time you suffer a consequence for not following through, it helps you stay on track. Once you have your standards in place, work according to them, not your moods. That will get you going in the right direction. Self–discipline is a quality that is won through practice

Failing Forward

THIS WEEK: Make a reasonable to–do list with goals for the week involving both your professional and your personal life. At the end of the week, check off what you actually accomplished. Why did some things happen and others not? Do you see areas where better discipline could help you accomplish more? What steps can you take to improve?

GOD'S PROMISE
TO LEADERS

Blessed is the man You choose,
And cause to approach You,
That he may dwell in Your courts.
We shall be satisfied with the goodness of Your house,
Of Your holy temple.

PSALM 65:4

A LEADER'S PROMISE
TO THE TEAM

I WILL NOT MAKE HASTY DECISIONS,
BUT WILL CAREFULLY SELECT THE
PEOPLE I INCLUDE ON OUR TEAM.
I WILL CONSIDER THE TEAM'S NEEDS AND
OPINIONS, NOT JUST MY OWN.

PICK THE RIGHT PEOPLE

Therefore, brethren, seek out from among you seven men
of good reputation, full of the Holy Spirit and wisdom,
whom we may appoint over this business.

ACTS 6:3

Red Auerbach, long-time president of the Boston Celtics, said, "How you select people is more important than how you manage them once they're on the job. If you start with the right people, you won't have problems later on." You have to begin with the right raw materials in order to create a winning team.

I want each of the people close to me to . . .

Know my heart. This takes time for both of us and desire on their part.

Be loyal to me. They are an extension of me and my work.

Be trustworthy. They must not abuse authority, power, or confidences.

Be discerning. They make decisions for me.

Have a servant's heart. They carry a heavy load because of my high demands.

Be a good thinker. Our two heads are better than my one.

Be able to follow through. They take authority and carry out the vision.

Have a great heart for God. My heart for God is my driving force in life.

Developing the Leaders Around You

An Investment for the Future

Most people recognize that investing in a team brings benefits to everyone on the team. Here are ten steps you can take to invest in your team.

1. Decide to build a team.
2. Gather the best team possible.
3. Pay the price to develop the team.
4. Do things together as a team.
5. Empower team members with responsibility and authority.
6. Give credit for success to the team.
7. Watch to see that the investment in the team is paying off.
8. Stop your investment in players who do not grow.
9. Create new opportunities for the team.
10. Give the team the best possible chance to succeed.

One of the great things about investing in a team is that it almost guarantees a high return for the effort, because a team can do so much more than individuals. Or as Rex Murphy, one of my conference attendees, told me: "Where there's a will there's a way; where there's a team, there's more than one way."

The 17 Indisputable Laws of Leadership

Recruit people who seize opportunities. The best people to take with you on the leadership journey don't simply sit back and wait for opportunities to come to them. They make it their responsibility to go out and find them. Good potential leaders don't rely on luck. Of the people around you, who always seems able to recognize opportunities and grab hold of them?

TAKE CARE OF THOSE CLOSEST TO YOU

*Just before the Passover Feast, Jesus knew that the time had come
to leave this world to go to the Father. Having loved his
dear companions, he continued to love them right to the end.*

JOHN 13:1 (MSG)

If you lead your team, you are responsible for making
sure that better players are joining the team than are
leaving. One of the ways you can facilitate that is to place
high value on the good people you already have on the
team. Every team has three groups of players.

Starters directly add value to the organization or
directly influence its course.

Bench players add value to the organization indirectly
or support the starters who do.

Inner–circle members are a core group within the starters,
and without them the team would fall apart.

Your job is to make sure each group is continually
developed so that bench players are able to step up to
become starters, and starters are able to step up to become
inner–circle members. If your treatment of key people
doesn't match their value, you run the risk of losing them.

The 17 Indisputable Laws of Teamwork

THIS WEEK: Who are your starters, bench players, and
inner–circle members? Are these people aware of their
importance? Have you made any bad investments in adding
to your team? What can you do to minimize the losses or
even turn things around to post some gains? What benefits
does each person bring to your team? What drawbacks?

GOD'S PROMISE
TO LEADERS

Now if you walk before Me as your father David
walked, in integrity of heart and in uprightness,
to do according to all that I have commanded
you, and if you keep My statutes and
My judgments, then I will establish the throne
of your kingdom over Israel forever, as I promised
David your father, saying, "You shall
not fail to have a man on the throne of Israel."

1 KINGS 9:4–5

A LEADER'S PROMISE
TO THE TEAM

I WILL TEACH MY SUCCESSORS WHAT I KNOW.
LEADERSHIP DOES NOT END WITH ME.

PREPARE YOUR SUCCESSOR

And everyone who was in distress, everyone who was in debt,
and everyone who was discontented gathered to [David].
So he became captain over them.
And there were about four hundred men with him.

1 SAMUEL 22:2

The men who David attracted while he fled from Saul eventually became like him. Some even killed giants as he did—showing that what you are is what you reproduce. Observe what David teaches us about his leadership:

1. David attracted men even without pursuing them.

2. David drew deep loyalty from them without ever trying to get it.

3. David transformed these men without disenchanting them over their initial state.

4. David fought alongside these men and turned them into winners.

Consider the astounding exploits of some of these men. Second Samuel 23:8 tells us that Adino slew 800 men with a spear in one battle (v. 8); Eleazar struck down the enemy until his hand clung to his sword (vv. 9, 10); Shammah defended a plot of ground against an enemy army (vv. 11, 12). David attracted men like him—souls in distress. He also reproduced men like him—warriors and conquerors.

The Maxwell Leadership Bible

CREATE A CLIMATE
FOR DEVELOPING LEADERS

We can conclude from the list of warriors who joined David in Ziklag that his ragtag team was diverse, loyal, and hungry for victory (1 Chronicles 12:38). So what did David do to reproduce his leadership in them?

1. *He was relational.* David's approachable manner enticed hundreds of misfits to serve him. David accepted anyone.

2. *He was resourceful.* David made the best of every situation. He resourced his team to become all it could be and enabled it to succeed.

3. *He was rewarding.* David quickly shared both rewards and recognition for victory. He affirmed his men and motivated them with words of encouragement and spoils from battle.

4. *He was respectable.* David modeled a leadership style that others wanted to imitate. Friends and foes alike respected him.

A leader passes the baton. King David was determined to ensure his legacy by preparing the next leader, Solomon, and committing him to the care of God (1 Chronicles 28–29). Look closely at what he did:

1. He rallied all the people together.

2. He affirmed God's choice of his successor.

3. He identified the great need for help.

4. He reminded the people of his own commitment.

5. He declared that the people were well on their way to the goal.

6. He asked for commitment.

The Maxwell Leadership Bible

LEADERSHIP TRANSITIONS CAN BE TRICKY

Transitions in leadership often cause significant problems for groups and organizations.

Solomon had to make some tough but crucial leadership decisions at the beginning of his reign. First, he had to deal with men scheming for power—one of his own brothers, Adonijah, even tried to set up his own kingdom (1 Kings 1:5). One by one, King Solomon discerned the loyalties of his associates, then removed all who refused to cooperate with him.

Solomon knew he could never work with renegades, no matter how influential or strategic they might seem. The young king ensured that his inner circle would include only loyal men who wanted to work with him.

David had seen these troubles brewing on the horizon. He knew he was placing his successor in a precarious leadership situation, but he confidently declared that Solomon would know what to do. David understood that those closest to Solomon would greatly hinder or improve his level of success. Solomon understood the same thing— and wisely acted on it.

The Maxwell Leadership Bible

THIS WEEK: Has your predecessor or superior affirmed your leadership? How do you affirm your successors or other team members? Is your team prepared for transition?

GOD'S PROMISE
TO LEADERS

Therefore do not worry, saying,
"What shall we eat?" or "What shall we drink?"
or "What shall we wear?" For after all these
things the Gentiles seek. For your heavenly Father
knows that you need all these things. But seek
first the kingdom of God and His righteousness,
and all these things shall be added to you.

MATTHEW 6:31–33

A LEADER'S PROMISE
TO THE TEAM

I WILL NOT LET LESS–SIGNIFICANT DETAILS
AND SITUATIONS GET IN THE WAY
OF OUR ACCOMPLISHING OUR CHIEF PURPOSE.

WEEK 43

PRIORITIZE YOUR LIFE

I have finished the work which You have given Me to do.

JOHN 17:4

Wwhen Peter was a young fisherman in Galilee, no one would have thought he was destined to become the passionate leader of a world movement. After all, he had almost no education and probably would have been happy to live the remainder of his life in obscurity. But God had something else in mind, and when Peter met Jesus, his priorities began to change.

Like many leaders, Peter had to learn how to put first things first. In fact, Scripture reveals a lot about the inconsistencies of his behavior and his many irrational decisions. But the more time Peter spent with Jesus, the more he learned the difference between mere activity and accomplishment.

Like Peter, great leaders sift through the many things that demand their time, and they discern not only what needs to be done first, but also what doesn't need to be done at all. That starts with a passion to excel. When you focus your passion on what's most important, your leadership climbs to new heights.

The 21 Most Powerful Minutes in a Leader's Day

WHEN YOUR PRIORITIES ARE RIGHT

Every leader must establish a list of priorities, then learn to put first things first. When Solomon became king of Israel, he was given the opportunity to ask God for anything (2 Chronicles 1:7–12). No doubt, King Solomon faced the same options we have today:

1. *Easy things first.* He could've chosen to focus on the easy tasks ahead of him.

2. *Fun things first.* He could've chosen to focus on riches or fame.

3. *Urgent things first.* He could've asked for help in building the temple.

4. *Hard things first.* He could've sought favor with those who didn't like him.

5. *First things first.* Instead, he chose to seek wisdom so he could glorify God.

Keep the main thing the main thing. Moses attempts this in Deuteronomy 6:5–7 by reminding the Israelites that their existence revolves around loving God. He also tells family leaders how to transfer truth to their children. Reggie Joiner notes the principles Moses develops:

1. Relationship comes before rules.

2. Truth must be in you before it can be in them.

3. Each day offers natural opportunities for teaching.

4. Repetition is the teacher's best friend.

Make use of all of these opportunities. Decide on issues you can discuss and ask questions of each other. Pray about your priorities together.

The Maxwell Leadership Bible

CHOOSE ACHIEVEMENT OVER AFFIRMATION

If you want to make an impact during your lifetime, you have to trade the praise you could receive from others for the things of value that you can accomplish.

A friend once explained something to me that illustrates this concept very well. He told me that as people catch crabs, they'll toss the crustaceans into a basket. If you have only one crab in the basket you need a lid to keep it from crawling out, but if you've got two or more, you don't. When there are several crabs, they will drag one another down so that none of them can get away.

A lot of unsuccessful people act the same way. They'll do things to keep others from getting ahead. But the good news is that if you observe someone trying to do that, you don't have to buy into their belief system. You can get out and stay out of the basket by refusing to be a crab.

Your Road Map for Success

THIS WEEK: In your interactions with people, ask yourself: "What priority is this serving? The importance of relationships? The value of our work? The growth of our faith? Other?" If the interaction is not benefiting a priority, what do you think you should do about it?

GOD'S PROMISE
TO LEADERS

For God has not given us a spirit of fear,
but of power and of love and of a sound mind.

2 TIMOTHY 1:7

A LEADER'S PROMISE
TO THE TEAM

I WILL NOT LET FEAR PARALYZE ME
FROM MAKING DECISIONS. I'D RATHER BREAK
NEW GROUND THAN LET THE STATUS QUO
BECOME OUR BURIAL GROUND.

RISK GREATNESS

Therefore, if anyone is in Christ, he is a new creation; old things have passed away; behold, all things have become new.

2 CORINTHIANS 5:17

S *tatus quo* is Latin for "the mess we're in." Leaders see what is, but they also have a vision for what could be. They are never content with things as they are. To be leading, by definition, is to be in front, breaking new ground, conquering new worlds, moving away from the status quo.

Dissatisfaction with the status quo does not mean having a negative attitude or grumbling. It has to do with a willingness to be different and to take risks. A person who refuses to risk change fails to grow. A leader who loves the status quo soon becomes a follower. Raymond Smith of the Bell Atlantic Corporation once remarked, "Administrators are easy to find and cheap to keep. Leaders—risk takers—are in very short supply. And ones with vision are pure gold."

Risk seems dangerous to many people because they are more comfortable with the old problems versus what it takes to come up with new solutions. The difference is attitude. When you seek out potential leaders, seek people who seek solutions.

Developing the Leaders Around You

Secure Leadership

Psalm 91 is one of the most comforting chapters in the Bible. It describes the security believers can enjoy through faith in God. Leaders especially can benefit from this set of promises. Study them and enjoy them:

Promise	Leader's Benefit
1. God's presence	1. It doesn't have to be lonely at the top.
2. God's protection	2. As you take initiative and risks, God keeps you safe.
3. God's peace	3. You don't have to feel insecure in unknown territory.
4. God's perspective	4. God gives an eternal view of life that keeps you steady.
5. God's provision	5. Regardless of your needs, God meets them.
6. God's power	6. In adversity, God delivers and helps you reach your goal.

Security is the foundation. We must feel secure even when people stop liking us, when funding drops, when morale dips, or when others reject us. If we don't feel secure, fear will eventually cause us to sabotage our leadership. David had covered up his sins after his affair with Bathsheba, so Nathan had to feel utterly secure in his plan of confrontation (2 Samuel 12:9). In God, we have every reason to feel secure as leaders.

The Maxwell Leadership Bible

Trade Your Fears for Faith in God

Brokenness involves removing inappropriate pride and self–reliance and building healthy God–reliance. God tamed Moses' self–reliance and pride in the desert, but to create trust He had to break the man's fears (Exodus 3:1–4:17). Moses dealt with different kinds of fear in his encounter with God:

Fears concerning himself. God responded by assuring Moses of his purpose.

Fears concerning God. God responded by overwhelming Moses with His presence.

Fears concerning others. God responded by demonstrating His power and commitment.

Fears concerning his ability. God responded by proving him with a partner, his brother, Aaron.

With his willfulness broken, his fears overcome, and his purpose affirmed, Moses finally placed himself in the hands of God (Exodus 4:20).

Life is filled with tradeoffs. Moses sacrificed his status and material possessions to prepare for his life purpose. And then to fulfill it, he had to sacrifice again, relinquishing the security and safety of obscurity in the desert. If you desire to lead, then you must be ready to make sacrifices.

The Maxwell Leadership Bible

This Week: Consider the risks that accompany your opportunities. Do you fear lack of resources or cooperation? Do you think the opportunities are beyond your capabilities? Are you secure in your leadership? What risks are you and your team willing to take? What assurance will help you risk more?

GOD'S PROMISE
TO LEADERS

*And my God shall supply all your need
according to His riches in glory by Christ Jesus.*

PHILIPPIANS 4:19

A LEADER'S PROMISE
TO THE TEAM

I WILL NOT ASK YOU TO SACRIFICE
MORE THAN I'M WILLING TO.
I WILL PLACE THE TEAM'S INTERESTS
ABOVE MY OWN PROFESSIONAL INTERESTS.

SACRIFICE TO STEP UP

My brethren, count it all joy when you fall into various trials.

JAMES 1:2

What price are you willing to pay to be a more effective leader?

One of the finest examples of sacrifice by a leader in the Bible can be seen in the life of Moses. He could easily be the "poster child" for leadership sacrifice. He grew up like a son of Pharaoh, a prince. As a boy, he enjoyed every privilege and pleasure of the palace.

Yet Moses risked all of that to try to help his people. And in fact, he lost everything. After murdering an Egyptian, he faced exile in the desert of Midian, and for forty years he lived with the sacrifice he had made before learning that God intended to use him as a leader. By then, Moses had undergone the breaking and remaking process required for him to be used by God.

As a leader you may not be asked to leave your country or give up all your possessions as Moses was. But you can be sure that leading others will have a price.

The 21 Most Powerful Minutes in a Leader's Day

GIVE UP YOUR RIGHTS

Have you been wronged? If so, you're faced with a decision. Are you going to spend your time and energy on what should have been, or are you going to focus on what can be?

Even when truth and justice are on your side, you may never be able to right your wrongs. Continually fighting for your rights will just make you resentful, angry, and negative. And besides, when you focus on your rights, you're often looking backward rather than forward.

When you stop worrying about your rights, you're released to move forward on the journey. You recognize the wrongs, but you forgive them and focus on what you can control—your responsibilities. This increases your energy, builds your potential, and improves your prospects.

Your Road Map for Success

As responsibilities increase, rights decrease. In a world of perks and privileges that accompany the climb to success, little thought is given to the responsibilities of the upward journey. John D. Rockefeller, Jr., said, "I believe that every right implies a responsibility; every opportunity, an obligation; every possession, a duty." Jesus said, "For everyone to whom much is given, from him much will be required; and to whom much has been committed, of him they will ask the more" (Luke 12:48).

Developing the Leader Within You

A Living Sacrifice

For even the Son of Man did not come to be served, but to serve, and to give His life a ransom for many.

MARK 10:45

Teams fail to reach their potential when they fail to pay the price for achieving it. If you lead a team, then one of the difficult things you must do is convince your teammates to sacrifice for the good of the group. The more talented the team members, the more difficult it may be to convince them to put the team first. Begin by modeling sacrifice. Show the team that you are willing to . . .
- Make financial sacrifices for the team.
- Keep growing for the sake of the team.
- Empower others for the sake of the team.
- Make difficult decisions for the sake of the team.

Once you have modeled a willingness to pay your own price for the potential of the team, you have the credibility to ask others to do the same. Then when you recognize sacrifices that teammates must make for the team, show them why and how to do it. Then praise their sacrifices greatly to their teammates.

The 21 Indisputable Laws of Teamwork

THIS WEEK: What have you sacrificed to be a leader? Are these the right sacrifices? What sacrifices are you asking of your team members?

GOD'S PROMISE
TO LEADERS

Teach the wise, and they will become even wiser;
teach good people, and they will learn even more.
Wisdom begins with respect for the LORD,
and understanding begins
with knowing the Holy One.

PROVERBS 9:9–10 (NCV)

A LEADER'S PROMISE
TO THE TEAM

I WILL SEEK OUT PEOPLE WHO CHALLENGE ME
TO STRETCH MY CURRENT ABILITIES,
SO THAT I CAN BE CONSTANTLY PUSHED TO
IMPROVE IN HOW I LEAD AND
SERVE THIS TEAM AND OUR MISSION.

SEEK PEOPLE
WHO STRETCH YOU

Take firm hold of instruction, do not let go;
Keep her, for she is your life.
Do not enter the path of the wicked,
And do not walk in the way of evil.
Avoid it, do not travel on it;
Turn away from it and pass on.

PROVERBS 4:13–15

A factor in your personal development comes in the area of your relationships with others. You can tell a lot about which direction your life is heading by looking at the people with whom you've chosen to spend your time and share your ideas. Their values and priorities impact the way you think and act. If they're positive people dedicated to growth, then their values and priorities will encourage you and reinforce your desire to grow.

It's not always comfortable to associate with people who are ahead of you in their growth, but it's always profitable. Try to cultivate relationships with those people who can help you grow, but don't think only in terms of what you can gain. Always bring something to the table yourself. You've got to make the relationship win–win or it won't last.

Your Road Map for Success

LEADERS WHO ATTRACT LEADERS

And men of all nations, from all the kings of the earth who had heard of his wisdom, came to hear the wisdom of Solomon.

1 KINGS 4:34

There are two kinds of leaders: those who attract followers and those who attract other leaders. People who team up only with followers will never be able to do anything beyond what they can personally touch or supervise. Look for leaders who attract other leaders.

LEADERS WHO ATTRACT FOLLOWERS . . .	LEADERS WHO ATTRACT LEADERS . . .
Need to be needed.	Want to be succeeded.
Want recognition.	Want to reproduce themselves.
Focus on others' weaknesses.	Focus on others' strengths.
Spend their time with others.	Invest their time in others.
Experience some success.	Experience incredible success.

To keep attracting better and better leaders, you will have to keep developing your own leadership ability.

Your Road Map for Success

Create room to grow. If you catch a small shark and confine it, it will stay a size proportionate to the aquarium in which it lives, but if you turn it loose in the ocean, it grows to its normal size. The same is true of potential leaders. Be a change agent who facilitates growth.

Developing the Leaders Around You

A Growing Community

They devoted themselves to the apostles' teaching and to the fellowship, to the breaking of bread and to prayer. Everyone was filled with awe, and many wonders and miraculous signs were done by the apostles. All the believers were together and had everything in common. . . . And the Lord added to their number daily those who were being saved.

Acts 2:42–44, 47 (NIV)

Your growth is affected by your environment. If your current circumstances do nothing to help you grow, you're going to have a hard time enlarging yourself to reach your potential. You must create an environment of growth in which . . .

1. Others are ahead of you.
2. You are still challenged.
3. Your focus is forward.
4. The atmosphere is affirming.
5. You are out of your comfort zone.
6. Others are growing.
7. There is a willingness to change.
8. Growth is modeled and expected.

A life of continual growth is never easy, but a good environment makes the swim upstream a little less difficult.

Your Road Map for Success

THIS WEEK: List some of the people in your life who stretch you. Do you need more such people? Are you attracting leaders to your team or are you attracting followers? What might you need to change?

GOD'S PROMISE
TO LEADERS

Trust in the LORD with all your heart,
And lean not on your own understanding;
In all your ways acknowledge Him,
And He shall direct your paths.

PROVERBS 3:5–6

A LEADER'S PROMISE
TO THE TEAM

I'M ENDEAVORING TO BE WISE AND
TO HEED WISE COUNSEL AS I LEAD THIS TEAM.
I WANT TO HEAR YOUR WISDOM, TOO.

SEEK WISDOM

The fear of the LORD is the beginning of knowledge,
But fools despise wisdom and instruction.

PROVERBS 1:7

Wisdom can be a leader's best friend, especially in times of decision. Suppose you find yourself in a large committee meeting in which a crucial decision must be made. The committee reaches an impasse and everything stops. Who will become the most influential person in that room? Answer: the one with the wisdom to draw a conclusion that not only works, but which receives the blessing of that committee.

Proverbs 1 describes wisdom as a woman crying out in the streets. What a beautiful picture! Wisdom does not hide herself, but shouts publicly! We must go out and find her and build a friendship with her: What can we learn about decision making from Proverbs?

1. The foundation for every decision is to honor and revere God.

2. We must build off our heritage and conscience: what values are we to embrace?

3. We must avoid the counsel of the ungodly.

4. We must pursue wisdom. What are the facts? What are the options?

5. We must move toward inward peace.

The Maxwell Leadership Bible

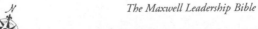

Near the beginning of Solomon's reign, Solomon asked for wisdom, and God answered abundantly (1 Kings 3:9). The Bible tells us that Solomon's wisdom exceeded that of any other man. His expansive mind explored the disciplines of botany, zoology, and music, and pondered topics ranging from economics to communication to love. The wisdom of King Solomon helped Israel prosper greatly. Solomon himself became the wealthiest king of his time.

But by the end of his reign, this brilliant king somehow forgot the first principle of wisdom: "The fear of the Lord is the beginning of wisdom" (Psalm 111:10). Only wisdom energized by a vibrant walk with God makes godly leaders.

How are godly leaders to think? Even good wisdom divorced from God can become a snare (Proverbs chapters 2 and 3), but godly leaders think:

Big. They realize God's vision is usually bigger than theirs.
Other people. They always include others in the mix.
Continually. They're not satisfied with today's answers.
Bottom line. They want to see results and fruit.
Continual growth. They want to keep improving.
Without lines. They let God outside of the box.
Victory. They want to see God's rule come to earth.
Intuitively. They have a sense of what will work.
Servanthood. They want to serve and add value to people.
Quickly. They evaluate quickly and see possible answers.

The Maxwell Leadership Bible

LEADERSHIP LESSONS FROM AN ANT

Go to the ant, you sluggard! Consider her ways and be wise,
which, having no captain, overseer or ruler, provides
her supplies in the summer, and gathers her food in the harvest.

PROVERBS 6:6–8

Do you want to make a difference? Then pay attention to the metaphor of the ant. It's amazing that one of the smallest of God's creatures can become one of His greatest teachers. The lessons the ant teaches us can be summarized this way:

A—Attitude of Initiative

Ants don't need a commander to tell them to get started.

N—Nature of Integrity

Ants work faithfully and need no outside accountability to keep them doing right.

T—Thirst for Industry

Ants work hard and will replace their anthill when it gets ruined.

S—Source of Insight

Ants store provisions in summer.

If we consider and learn from the ways of the ant, we can grow wise.

The Maxwell Leadership Bible

THIS WEEK: List the wise people in your life. How many are your leaders? How many are your followers or peers? Why do you think these people are wise? How wise do others think you are? Do you have a personal plan for growing in wisdom?

GOD'S PROMISE
TO LEADERS

A wise man is strong,
Yes, a man of knowledge increases strength;
For by wise counsel you will wage your own war,
And in a multitude of counselors there is safety.

PROVERBS 24:5–6

A LEADER'S PROMISE
TO THE TEAM

I WILL FOCUS MY ENERGIES ON
OUR STRENGTHS. THIS WILL HELP US
GROW FAR MORE THAN IF I POUR RESOURCES
INTO BOLSTERING OUR WEAKNESSES.

SPEND TIME WITH YOUR BEST

Now after six days Jesus took Peter, James, and John,
and led them up on a high mountain apart by themselves.

MARK 9:2

Years ago I learned the Pareto Principle and began applying it to my life. It's a useful tool for determining priorities for any person's life or for any organization.

THE PARETO PRINCIPLE
20 percent of your priorities will give you
80 percent of your production
IF you spend your time, energy, money, and personnel on the
top 20 percent of your priorities.

Every leader needs to understand the Pareto Principle in the area of people oversight and leadership. For example, 20 percent of the people in an organization will be responsible for 80 percent of the company's success. The following strategy will enable a leader to increase the productivity of an organization.

1. Determine your top 20 percent producers.

2. Spend 80 percent of your "people time" with the top 20 percent.

3. Spend 80 percent of your personal development dollars on the top 20 percent.

4. Ask the top 20 percent to do on–the–job training for the next 20 percent.

Developing the Leader Within You

BRING OUT THEIR BEST

Many organizations today fail to tap into their potential. Why? Because the only reward they give their employees is a paycheck. In successful organizations a worker receives not only his paycheck, but he is also nurtured by the people he works for. This nurturing has the ability to transform people's lives.

I use the "BEST" acronym as a reminder that my people need me to . . .

Believe in them
Encourage them
Share with them
Trust them

Nurturing makes people more productive, and it creates a strong emotional and professional foundation within workers who have leadership potential. Later, using training and development, a leader can be built on that foundation.

Developing the Leaders Around You

As you train others . . . The apostle Paul began a miniature seminary in Ephesus, and he also trained men in the lecture hall of Tyrannus (Acts 19:8–10). As he mentored students, Paul remained committed to the people, to the process, and to the purpose. Consider how we can do the same as we develop others:

Be familiar with your strengths and weaknesses.

Know the people you wish to develop.

Clearly define the goals and assignments.

Allow them to watch you serve and lead.

Hold them accountable for their work.

Give them the freedom to fail.

The Maxwell Leadership Bible

HOPE FLOATS

Therefore my heart is glad, and my glory rejoices;
My flesh also will rest in hope.

PSALM 16:9

How do most people feel when they're around you? Do they feel small and insignificant, or do they believe in themselves and have great hope about what they can become?

The key to how you treat people lies in how you think about them. It's a matter of attitude. What you believe is revealed by how you act. Johann Wolfgang von Goethe said: "Treat a man as he appears to be and you make him worse. But treat a man as if he already were what he potentially could be, and you make him what he should be."

Hope is perhaps the greatest gift you can give another person as the result of nurturing, because even if people fail to see their own significance, they still have a reason to keep trying and striving to reach their potential in the future.

Becoming a Person of Influence

THIS WEEK: Consider the potentials of your people. Leaders are meant to help others become the people God created them to be. They are called to discover the hidden, encourage the uncertain, develop the untrained, and empower the powerless. Just as Jesus sees potential in you, if you are a leader, He wants you to find and develop that potential in others.

GOD'S PROMISE
TO LEADERS

Blessed are the undefiled in the way,
Who walk in the law of the LORD!
Blessed are those who keep His testimonies,
Who seek Him with the whole heart!
They also do no iniquity;
They walk in His ways.

PSALM 119:1–3

A LEADER'S PROMISE
TO THE TEAM

THESE ARE OUR GOALS.
I'VE SUBMITTED THEM TO GOD,
AND I'M COMMITTED
TO KEEPING US ON TARGET.

STAY THE COURSE

Do not turn from it to the right hand or to the left,
that you may prosper wherever you go.

JOSHUA 1:7

To be intentional means working with purpose, making every action count. Successful leaders are intentional. They know what they're doing and why they're doing it. To become more intentional, do the following:

1. *Have a purpose worth living for.* Willis R. Whitney, the first director of General Electric's research laboratory, observed, "Some men have thousands of reasons why they cannot do what they want to, when all they need is one reason why they can."

2. *Know your strengths and weaknesses.* Playing to your strengths rekindles your passions and renews your energy.

3. *Prioritize your responsibilities.* Once you know the "why" of your life, it becomes much easier to figure out the "what" and "when."

4. *Learn to say no.* You can't accomplish much without focus. If you try to do every good thing that comes your way, you won't excel at what you were made to do.

5. *Commit yourself to long–term achievement.* Most victories in life are achieved through small incremental wins sustained over time.

The 17 Essential Qualities of a Team Player

Set Good Goals

The number of people today who lack a strong sense of purpose is astounding. Pulitzer–winning writer Katherine Anne Porter observed: "I am appalled at the aimlessness of most people's lives. Fifty percent don't pay any attention to where they are going; forty percent are undecided and will go in any direction. Only ten percent know what they want, and even all of them don't go toward it."

Goals give you something concrete to focus on, and that has a positive impact on your actions. Goals help us focus our attention on our purpose and make it our dominant aspiration. And as philosopher–poet Ralph Waldo Emerson said, "The world makes way for the man who knows where he is going."

Use the following guidelines to keep your goals on target. Goals must be . . .

- Written
- Personal
- Specific
- Achievable
- Measurable
- Time–sensitive

Your Road Map for Success

Effective leaders don't drift. The apostle Paul had a plan to reach the Roman Empire in his lifetime (1 Corinthians 16:5–9). He focused on the metropolitan areas, knowing that well–trained followers would bring God's message to the smaller towns and villages. Leaders can do anything, but they can't do everything. What kind of plan do you have?

The Maxwell Leadership Bible

THE DANGER OF TOO MANY PURSUITS

Whatever my eyes desired I did not keep from them.
I did not withhold my heart from any pleasure,
For my heart rejoiced in all my labor;
And this was my reward from all my labor.
Then I looked on all the works that my hands had done
And on the labor in which I had toiled;
And indeed all was vanity and grasping for the wind.
There was no profit under the sun.

ECCLESIASTES 2:10–11

Solomon fervently pursued several unrelated goals in a vain attempt to satisfy himself. Eventually, he reached a high level of success but still felt empty. The axiom remains true: "If you chase two rabbits, both will escape."

How about you? Do you have a way of determining your focus, based on what really matters or what really counts? When faced with a decision, ask yourself:

Is this consistent with my priorities?
Is this within my area of competence?
Can someone else do it better?
What do my trusted friends say?
Do I have the time?

The Maxwell Leadership Bible

THIS WEEK: Write your top three goals for your business, for your family, and for yourself. Are these goals truly in line with your priorities? Do members of your team understand the goals? Are your goals high enough? Do you have a plan of attack?

GOD'S PROMISE
TO LEADERS

Now, therefore, you are no longer strangers and foreigners, but fellow citizens with the saints and members of the household of God, having been built on the foundation of the apostles and prophets, Jesus Christ Himself being the chief cornerstone, in whom the whole building, being fitted together, grows into a holy temple in the Lord, in whom you also are being built together for a dwelling place of God in the Spirit.

EPHESIANS 2:19–22

A LEADER'S PROMISE
TO THE TEAM

I WILL REMIND US OF OUR TEAM GOALS,
AND I WILL CONSISTENTLY ENCOURAGE AND
REWARD TEAM EFFORTS.

TEAMWORK MAKES THE DREAM WORK

*But God composed the body, having given greater honor to that
part which lacks it, that there should be no schism in the body,
but that the members should have the same care for one
another. And if one member suffers, all the members suffer with
it; or if one member is honored, all the members rejoice with it.*

1 CORINTHIANS 12:24–26

I f your team members believe in the goals of the team
and begin to develop genuine trust in one another, they
will be in a position to demonstrate true teamwork. Notice
that I mention the team members will be in a position to
demonstrate true teamwork. That does not necessarily
mean that they will do it.

For there to be teamwork, several things must happen.
First, team members must genuinely believe that the value
of the team's success is greater than the value of their own
individual interests. Second, personal sacrifice must be
encouraged and then rewarded—by the team leader and
the other members of the team. As this happens, the people
will identify themselves more and more with the team, and
they will recognize that individualism wins trophies, but
teamwork wins pennants.

Developing the Leaders Around You

Build Relationships to Build the Team

Teams that don't bond, can't build. Why? Because they never become a cohesive unit. Why do wounded soldiers strive to rejoin their buddies on the battlefield? Because after you work and live with people, you soon realize that your survival depends on one another. For a team to be successful, the teammates have to know that they will look out for one another. When a team member cares about no one but himself, the whole team suffers.

I have found that one of the best ways to get members of a team to care about one another is to get them together outside of a work context in order to build relationships. Every year in our organization we plan retreats and other events that put our people together in social settings. And during those times, we also make sure that they spend part of their time with staff members they don't really know very well. That way they're not only building relationships, but they're being prevented from developing cliques.

Developing the Leaders Around You

Teammates must collaborate. Becoming a collaborative team player requires a change in four areas:

1. *Perception.* See teammates as collaborators, not competitors.

2. *Attitude.* Be supportive, not suspicious, of teammates.

3. *Focus.* Concentrate on the team, not yourself.

4. *Results.* Create great victories though multiplication.

The 17 Essential Qualities of a Team Player

LIKE A ROCK

Dependability is important to every team's success. Everyone on the team knows upon whom they can and can't depend. Allow me to give you what I consider to be the essence of dependability:

1. *Pure motives.* If someone on the team continually puts themselves and their agenda ahead of what's best for the team, they have proven themselves to be undependable. When it comes to teamwork, motives matter.

2. *Responsibility.* While motivation addresses why people are dependable, responsibility indicates that they want to be dependable.

3. *Sound thinking.* Dependability means more than just wanting to take responsibility. That desire must also be coupled with good judgment to be of real value to the team.

4. *Consistent contribution.* The final quality of a dependable team player is consistency. If you can't depend on teammates all the time, then you can't really depend on them any of the time. Consistency takes a depth of character that enables people to follow through no matter how tired, distracted, or overwhelmed they are.

The 17 Essential Qualities of a Team Player

THIS WEEK: Upon whom do you depend? Do these people know how much confidence you have in them? Do the members of your team know they can depend on you? Where among the team members—including yourself—has dependability been tested and found wanting? Where has dependability held firm? How did your team recover after the slip in dependability?

GOD'S PROMISE
TO LEADERS

Those who lead good people to do wrong
will be ruined by their own evil,
but the innocent will be rewarded with good things.

PROVERBS 28:10 (NCV)

A LEADER'S PROMISE
TO THE TEAM

I WILL USE MY INFLUENCE
TO LEAD US IN THE RIGHT WAY
AND HELP US GROW.

UNDERSTAND INFLUENCE

"But only speak a word, and my servant will be healed.
For I also am a man under authority, having soldiers under me.
And I say to this one, 'Go,' and he goes; and to another,
'Come,' and he comes; and to my servant, 'Do this,' and he does it."

MATTHEW 8:8–9

A person's ability to make things happen in and through others depends entirely on their ability to lead them.

If your dream is big and will require the teamwork of a lot of people, then any potential leaders you select to go with you on the journey will need to be people of influence. After all, that's what leadership is—influence. And when you think about it, all leaders have two things in common: They're going somewhere, and they're able to persuade others to go with them.

As you look at the people around you, consider the following:

Who influences them?

Whom do they influence?

Is their influence increasing or decreasing?

To be a good judge of potential leaders, don't just see the person—see all the people who that person influences. The greater the influence, the greater the leadership potential and the ability to get others to work with you to accomplish your dream.

Your Road Map for Success

OBSERVE YOUR INFLUENCE

It takes more than talk to keep workers in line;
mere words go in one ear and out the other.

PROVERBS 29:19 (MSG)

All of us are leading in some areas, while in other areas we are being led. No one is excluded from being a leader or a follower. Realizing your potential as a leader is your responsibility.

The chief influencer of any group is quite easy to discover. Just observe the people as they gather. If an issue is to be decided, who is the person whose opinion seems most valuable? Who do others watch the most when the issue is being discussed? With whom do people quickly agree? Most importantly, who do the others follow? Answers to these questions will help you discern who the real leader is in a group.

Developing the Leader Within You

Make a good impression. If people perceive that you are positive and trustworthy and have admirable qualities, then they will seek you as an influencer in their lives. When you first meet people, you have no influence with them. If someone they trust makes the introduction, you can temporarily "borrow" some of that person's influence. But quickly you either build or bust that influence by your actions.

Becoming a Person of Influence

EXTENDING YOUR INFLUENCE

One of the greatest lessons I've ever learned is that the people closest to me determine my level of success or failure. On my fortieth birthday I discovered that my influence and productivity were growing only where I had identified potential leaders and developed them. My intention in developing leaders had been to help them improve themselves, but I found that I was also benefiting greatly. Spending time with them had been like investing. They had grown, and at the same time I had reaped incredible dividends. That's when I realized that if I was to make it to the next level, I was going to have to extend myself through others. I would find leaders and pour my life into them, and as they improved, so would I.

Your Road Map for Success

THIS WEEK: Integrity is critical if you want to become an influencer. It is the foundation upon which many other qualities are built, such as respect, dignity, and trust. "Good leaders abhor wrongdoing of all kinds; sound leadership has a moral foundation" (Proverbs 16:12). Are you a person of integrity? Where do you need to strengthen your foundation? Do you surround yourself with people of integrity?

Becoming a Person of Influence

GOD'S PROMISE
TO LEADERS

As for God, His way is perfect;
The word of the LORD is proven;
He is a shield to all who trust in Him.

PSALM 18:30

A LEADER'S PROMISE
TO FOLLOWERS
WE HAVE A VISION. THIS IS A
CHALLENGE WORTHY OF OUR CAPABILITIES
AND COMMITMENT. WE CAN DO THIS!

VISION BRINGS VICTORY

*Therefore, King Agrippa, I was not disobedient to the
heavenly vision, but declared first to those in Damascus and in
Jerusalem, and throughout all the region of Judea, and
then to the Gentiles, that they should repent,
turn to God, and do works befitting repentance.*

ACTS 26:19–20

The apostle Paul's vision on the road to Damascus became the captivating force behind his success as a leader. The apostle teaches us the power of a vision. God was Paul's leader, and His vision for Paul accomplished a number of things.

It stopped him. Vision allows us to see ourselves. We see things not as they are, but as we are.

It sent him. Vision allows us to see others. We feel compelled to act.

It strengthened him. Vision enables us to continue despite struggles and lack of resources.

It stretched him. Vision gives us conviction to stand, confidence to speak, and compassion to share.

It satisfied him. Obedience to this vision motivates us to act. It fulfills us.

The Maxwell Leadership Bible

Checklist for Casting the Vision

As a leader, you carry the responsibility for communicating the team's vision and keeping it before the people continually. That's not necessarily easy. People need to be shown the team's vision clearly, creatively, and continually. Whenever I cast vision with my team, I use the following checklist.

1. *Clarity* brings understanding to the vision.
2. *Connectedness* brings the past, present, and future together.
3. *Purpose* brings direction to the vision.
4. *Goals* bring targets to the vision.
5. *Honesty* brings integrity to the vision and credibility to the vision caster.
6. *Stories* bring relationships to the vision.
7. *Challenge* brings stretching to the vision.
8. *Passion* brings fuel to the vision.
9. *Modeling* brings accountability to the vision.
10. *Strategy* brings process to the vision.

With this checklist, your team will find the vision more accessible and will more readily buy in to it.

We need a good challenge. A truly great vision speaks to what team members can become if they truly live out their values and work according to their highest standards. Without a challenge, many people tend to fall or fade away. If you can see vision for your team, then your team has a reasonably good chance at success. Vision gives team members direction and confidence, two things they cannot do without.

The 17 Indisputable Laws of Teamwork

Without Buy–In, the Vision Perishes

All leaders have vision. But not all people who possess vision are leaders. I've known a lot of would–be leaders who possessed vision but lacked the ability to get people to buy in to them. A compelling vision alone will not make someone a leader. Nor will a great vision automatically be fulfilled simply because it is compelling or valuable. Followers need to buy in to the leader.

Once Gideon possessed the vision to deliver Israel from its enemies, he wasn't done. He still needed to get the people to buy in to his leadership. After time and effort, so many people bought into Gideon's leadership that God had to send a bunch of them home. If you look at the way Gideon progressed from being an obscure member of a minor clan to a leader of the Northern tribes, you can see his influence growing the way ripples do when a pebble is dropped in quiet water.

The 21 Most Powerful Minutes in a Leader's Day

THIS WEEK: Put your vision into words. If you can't capture the vision on paper, then you probably haven't defined it well enough. Is your vision appropriate for your current team? How might you need to adapt the vision, the team, or yourself?

TAKE ME TO YOUR LEADER

Now I saw heaven opened, and behold, a white horse.
And He who sat on him was called Faithful and True, and in
righteousness He judges and makes war . . . And the armies
in heaven, clothed in fine linen, white and clean, followed Him
on white horses . . . And He Himself will rule them with
a rod of iron. He Himself treads the winepress of the fierceness
and wrath of Almighty God. And He has on His robe and
on His thigh a name written: King of Kings and Lord of Lords.

Revelation 19:11, 14–16

In this passage from the last book of the Bible, John, the writer of Revelation, is describing Jesus Christ, the one who will ultimately rule the world at the end of time. In most of the Bible, Jesus is described as a humble and lowly servant. He healed the sick. He forgave the sinful. He washed the feet of fishermen, tax collectors, and the man who would betray him. And he meekly submitted to torture and gruesome death on the cross.

But make no mistake. Jesus is no weakling! In the book of Revelation, we see another side of His character and leadership. He is a captain of war who can rally huge heavenly armies to defeat a strong and bitter enemy. And He not only wins the day, but all eternity. That is a mark of great leaders. They have the strength to conquer, yet they stoop to help the weak and raise them up to join in the victory.

I believe in leadership. I've dedicated more than thirty years of my life to teaching it. But as Jesus Himself said, "What profit is it to a man if he gains the whole world, and loses his own soul?" (Matthew 16:26). If you do not have a relationship with the King of kings, Jesus Christ, then I want to invite you to enter into one. If you acknowledge that Jesus is the Son of God, repent of your sins, ask for forgiveness, and invite Jesus into your heart, you will be saved, and he will become your Lord of lords. And you will join Him, the ultimate leader, in eternity.

INDEX

ACKNOWLEDGEMENTS

Leadership Promises for Your Work Week is adapted from John C. Maxwell's *Leadership Promises for Every Day* (Nashville: Thomas Nelson, Inc., 2003).

Grateful acknowledgment is made to the following publishers for permission to reprint this copyrighted material. All copyrights are held by the author, John. C. Maxwell.

The Maxwell Leadership Bible (Nashville: Thomas Nelson, Inc, 1982).

Developing the Leader Within You (Nashville: Thomas Nelson, Inc., 2001).

Developing the Leaders Around You (Nashville: Thomas Nelson, Inc., 1995).

The 21 Irrefutable Laws of Leadership (Nashville: Thomas Nelson, Inc., 2002).

The 21 Indispensable Qualities of a Leader (Nashville: Thomas Nelson, Inc., 1999).

Becoming a Person of Influence (Nashville: Thomas Nelson, Inc., 1997).

The 21 Most Powerful Minutes in a Leader's Day (Nashville: Thomas Nelson, Inc., 2000).

Failing Forward (Nashville: Thomas Nelson, Inc., 2000).

The 17 Indisputable Laws of Teamwork (Nashville: Thomas Nelson, Inc., 2001).

The 17 Essential Qualities of a Team Player (Nashville: Thomas Nelson, Inc., 2002).

Your Road Map for Success (Nashville: Thomas Nelson, Inc., 2002).

About the Author

John C. Maxwell is an internationally recognized leadership expert, speaker, and author who has sold over 12 million books. His organizations have trained more than one million leaders worldwide. Dr. Maxwell is the founder of Injoy Stewardship Services and EQUIP. Every year he speaks to Fortune 500 companies, international government leaders, and organizations as diverse as the United States Military Academy at West Point and the National Football League. A *New York Times, Wall Street Journal,* and *Business Week* best-selling author, Maxwell was one of twenty-five authors named to Amazon.com's 10th Anniversary Hall of Fame. Two of his books, *The 21 Irrefutable Laws of Leadership* and *Developing the Leader Within You,* have each sold over a million copies.

NOTES

Notes

NOTES

NOTES

NOTES